1 MONTH OF
FREE
READING

at

www.ForgottenBooks.com

By purchasing this book you are eligible for one month membership to ForgottenBooks.com, giving you unlimited access to our entire collection of over 1,000,000 titles via our web site and mobile apps.

To claim your free month visit:

www.forgottenbooks.com/free440879

ISBN 978-0-484-41885-0
PIBN 10440879

Jaffrey Centennial.

PROCEEDINGS

OF THE

Centennial Celebration

OF THE

One Hundredth Anniversary

OF THE INCORPORATION OF THE

Town of Jaffrey, N. H.

AUGUST 20, 1873.

PREPARED FOR PUBLICATION BY THE COMMITTEE OF ARRANGEMENTS.

WINCHENDON:
PRINTED BY F. W. WARD & CO.
1873.

23222

PRELIMINARY PROCEEDINGS.

A T the Annual Town Meeting, March 8th, 1870, pursuant to an article in the warrant, voted that John Fox, Joseph P. Frost, Addison Prescott, David C. Chamberlain and Rufus Case, be a committee to collect facts in reference to making preparations for a Centennial celebration August 17th, 1873, and said committee appointed, as assistants, one person in each School District, viz : — Benjamin Cutter, Geo. A. Underwood, Addison J. Adams, Ambrus W. Spaulding, Lewis L. Pierce, Franklin H. Cutter, Clarence S. Bailey, Joseph W. Fassett, John S. Lawrence, John Frost, Benj. Pierce, Benjamin Prescott and Lewis S. Jaquith.

At the annual Town Meeting, March 12th, 1872, consequent to an article in the warrant, a vote was passed to celebrate the one hundredth anniversary of the incorporation of the Town, and chose John Fox, Addison Prescott, Benjamin Pierce, Lewis S. Jaquith, Julius Cutter and Franklin H. Cutter a committee to carry the same into effect.

November 5th, 1872, the town voted that the committee chosen to make the necessary preparation for the approaching Centennial anniversary of the town, be authorized to fill all vacancies which may occur in said committee.

Subsequently John Fox and Lewis S. Jaquith withdrew, and the vacancies were filled by George A. Underwood and Lewis L. Pierce.

The committee organized by choosing Lewis L. Pierce, corresponding Secretary and Clerk ; Franklin H. Cutter, Chairman, and Julius Cutter, Treasurer ; commencing their duties by engaging an orator and poet.

At the Annual Meeting, March 11th, 1873, the town voted to celebrate its centennial anniversary at the centre of the town; also, that the Committee of Arrangements and Selectmen be a committee to determine in what way the collation should be provided, — said committee deciding it should be furnished gratuitously, and to carry the same into effect, the committee of arrangements appointed Mr. & Mrs. Joseph W. Fassett, Mr. & Mrs. Alfred Sawyer, Mr. & Mrs. John A. Cutter, Mr. & Mrs. John S. Dutton, Mr. Henry Chamberlain, Mr. & Mrs. Frederic Spaulding, Mr. & Mrs. Addison J. Adams, Mr. & Mrs. Ambrus W. Spaulding, Mr. & Mrs. Daniel P. Adams, Mr. & Mrs. Marshall C. Adams, Mr. & Mrs. Levi E. Brigham, Mr. & Mrs. Abram B. Davis, Mr. & Mrs. Benjamin F. Lawrence, Mr. & Mrs. John E. Baldwin, Mr. &. Mrs. Lucius A. Cutter, Mr. & Mrs. Joel H. Poole, Mr. & Mrs. Joseph Davis, Mr. & Mrs. Henry M. Stearns, Mr. Samuel Jewell, Mr. Fred J. Lawrence, Mr. & Mrs. Michael D. Fitzgerald, Mr. & Mrs. Edward H. Crowe, Mr. & Mrs. Selah Lovejoy, Mr. &. Mrs. Hosea B. Aldrich, Mr. & Mrs. David A. Cutler, Mr. & Mrs. Sylvester P. Towne, Mr. & Mrs. Oliver H. Brown, Mr. & Mrs. Liberty Lower, and Mr. & Mrs. Thos. Upton as a soliciting and table committee, who performed their duties in a highly commendable manner, and the result was, the multitude that came, were bountifully supplied with substantial and delicate food, with an abundance of ice-water. Tea, coffee, lemonade, foaming soda &c., were obtained by passing into side tents.

The committee of arrangements appointed James S. Lacy, Austin E. Spaulding and Benjamin Pierce to arrange a choir of singers for the centennial day; also made choice of Franklin H. Cutter, Esq., President; Dr. John Fox, Peter Upton, Esq., Col. Samuel Ryan, Ex-Consul Chas. H. Powers, Capt. John A. Cutter, Henry C. French, Alfred Sawyer, Ambrus W. Spaulding, Col. James L. Bolster, Vice-Presidents; Capt. George A. Underwood, Marshal; he appointing Joseph W. Fassett, Jonas C. Rice, Henry B. Wheeler, Esq., Aids, for the day.

The expenses of the celebration were paid by subscription, as will herein be shown.

A letter of invitation was issued by the committee, printed on eight hundred Postal Cards, copied as follows :

"JAFFREY CENTENNIAL."

" The One Hundredth Anniversary of the Incorporation of the Town of Jaffrey, N. H., occurs this year. It is proposed to celebrate the event on the twentieth day of August, with appropriate ceremonies. The Sons and Daughters of Jaffrey, and all former residents are cordially invited to be present and take part in commemorating the day."

FRANKLIN H. CUTTER,
ADDISON PRESCOTT,
BENJAMIN PIERCE,   COMMITTEE
JULIUS CUTTER,   OF
GEO. A. UNDERWOOD,   ARRANGEMENTS.
LEWIS L. PIERCE,

JAFFREY, JULY 26th, 1873.

This letter was, by the committee, sent to all parts of the country, to former residents of the town.

As the one hundredth anniversary of the incorporation of the town occurred on Sunday, August 17th, it was decided to celebrate on the Wednesday following.

The day proved favorable. At an early hour, from all quarters, crowds assembled at the place of meeting to the number of five thousand or more. Many friendly and hearty greetings were passed between those who had long been separated, and were now permitted to take each other by the hand.

A mammoth tent covering 150 by 60 feet of ground, was erected in close connection to the " old town house." An ample platform, measuring forty by fifteen feet, was covered by a nice piano, large reporters' table, and settees for one hundred and fifty persons ; the " auditorium " proper having seats for more than three thousand people.

"THE DAY'S DOINGS."

The component parts of a long and eye-pleasing procession — Captain George A. Underwood, Chief Marshal; J. W. Fassett, J. C. Rice, H. B. Wheeler, Assistants—formed at three different points. Having been brought together on time, it moved from the vicinity of J. T. Bigelow's store at 9 A. M., in the following order: 1 — Peterboro' Cavalry Company, Capt. D. M. White, 55 men; 2 — East Jaffrey Cornet Band, G. W. Capen, Leader, 20 pieces; 3 — Contoocook Fire Engine Company, Liberty Town, Foreman, 40 uniforms; 4—President of the day, Orator, Toastmaster, and Chaplain; 5—The Vice-Presidents; 6—Committee of Arrangements; 7 — Invited guests expected to respond to sentiments; 8 — Choir, marshaled by J. S. Lacy, 30 strong; 9 — Loyal Veterans, Lieut. Wm. Robbins, Commander; 10 — Four horse wagon with four generations of the Rice family, and a banner lettered " Mrs. Dorcas Rice — 104 yrs.— the oldest lady in New Hampshire;" 11 — 23 young ladies (conducted by John E. Baldwin) representing Cheshire County by carrying elegant banners, each respectively inscribed with the name of a single town; 12 — Teachers and scholars of thirteen district schools with handsomely mottoed and numbered standards; 13 — Citizens generally. Having marched and counter-marched perhaps a half mile, the procession (except the Cavalry which left for East Jaffrey depot to escort soon-to-arrive members of the Boston city government) entered the tent which proved of insufficient capacity for the occasion, many hundreds being obliged, *nolens volens*, to remain outside. Precisely at ten o'clock, Chief Marshal Underwood felicitously introduced Franklin H. Cutter, Esq., President of the day, who forcibly enunciated the subjoined

ADDRESS OF WELCOME.

LADIES AND GENTLEMEN :—I congratulate you upon this eventful occasion — this celebration of the One Hundredth Anniversary of the Incorporation of the Town of Jaffrey. I congratulate you at our re-union under so favorable circumstances here at the foot of old time-worn Monadnock. Since that incorporation day, one hundred years ago, which bears *the* prominent place on the pages of our town's history, this earth has made thirty-six thousand, five hundred and twenty-four daily revolutions, and ofttimes has the morning sun kissed the *brow* of Grand Old Monadnock, nature's pride, lighting up the hills with rosy glow, then beaming down into the valleys draped with shadows till nature has changed her sable robe of night for that of the sun's molten golden light. Then came the mid-day with all its meridian glory, and as many times that sun has cast its evening shades on the hill-sides and left its last ray on that same mountain's brow, reflecting upon the sky most gorgeous hues of flame-color and crimson, imperceptibly deepening into the purple tinge of evening.

To the Sons and Daughters of those who have occupied these granite hills in days gone by — the statesman, the lawyer, the preacher, the doctor — and to all, those in every station of life, coming from the colder climes of the North, from the South where the orange trees in fragrance bloom, from the East where the angry Atlantic lashes the rock-bound shore with its turbulent waters, from the broad prairies of the West, dotted here and there with mammoth fields of wheat, corn and other grain, on to the shores of the mighty Pacific, — we give you all a most cordial welcome upon this festival day to our hearths where the fire goeth not out and hospitality ever reigneth; to the homes of your ancestors, the places of your childhood about which so many tender recollections cluster, as we sing

> "How dear to my heart are the scenes of my childhood,
>   When fond recollection presents them to view;
> The orchard, the meadow, the deep tangled wild-wood,
>   And every loved spot which my infancy knew;
> The wide spreading pond, and the mill that stood by it,
>   The bridge, and the rock where the cataract fell;
> The cot of my father, the dairy-house nigh it,
>   And e'en the rude bucket that hung in the well."

We welcome you back to witness the beautiful scenery of Jaffrey; to look upon our mountain in all its magnificence and grandeur; to follow its winding streams and from their pure waters catch the spotted trout suited to the most fastidious taste; to walk in the old grave-yard and gaze upon those tomb-stones which denote the spot where our fathers rest. Our neighbors and friends we welcome *you* to participate in the festivities of this occasion. We give you all a friendly grip of the hand, invite you to take part in this Centennial Celebration and thank God that we are here to speak one to another of days gone by and spend a short time together with the memories of Auld Lang Syne. May blessings rest upon this day and the town of Jaffrey, her sons and daughters, through all coming centuries.

Applause having subsided, the band played "Keller's American Hymn" in good style, when Rev. Rufus Case, pastor of the First Congregational Church at Jaffrey Centre, offered an excellent prayer, after which the choir, led by Prof. Geo. Foster, of Keene, harmoniously vocalized an original

"SONG OF WELCOME."

BY MISS ALMEDA M. SMITH.

Back from the prairied West,
 Dear kindred, welcome home;
This native soil you blest,
 Ere tempted far to roam.
Welcome to Jaffrey's granite hills,
Her rocky vales and sparkling rills.

Back from the South's fair land,
 Back from the holly's shade,
Welcome to join our band,
 From every hill and glade.
Welcome to Jaffrey's granite hills,
Her rocky vales and sparkling rills.

O'er ocean's waters blue
 We bid you come once more;
Our hearts are faithful, true,
 As in the days of yore.
Welcome to Jaffrey's granite hills,
Her rocky vales and sparkling rills.

Come, join our festal throng,
 'Neath stern Monadnock's brow;
Our hearts to day are strong

In friendship pure, I trow.
Welcome to Jaffrey's granite hills,
Her rocky vales and sparkling rills.

A century ago
 Your fathers trod this soil;
The gray old rocks we know
 Bear witness of their toil.
Welcome to Jaffrey's granite hills,
Her rocky vales and sparkling rills.

With thankful hearts we bow
 To God, our Father, Friend,
That here we meet e'en now,
 And our glad greetings blend.
Welcome to Jaffrey's granite hills,
Her rocky vale and sparkling rills.

We welcome you again
 To your dear native land;
Join in our sweet refrain
 With voice and heart and hand.
Welcome to Jaffrey's granite hills,
Her rocky vales and sparkling rills.

President Cutter then came forward and said, LADIES AND GENTLEMEN :— It is with great satisfaction that I have the pleasure of introducing to you as Orator of the Day, a native of Jaffrey. The venerable gentleman has lived nearly half a score of years more than the number allotted to man, and is thoroughly acquainted with the early history of this town. He has served his native State, New Hampshire, as Chief Justice for a series of years, and to him the jurists of our State have looked for counsel. He has also been a guiding star in the legal profession of our sister State where he now resides. Well can we afford to listen at this time to the HON. JOEL PARKER, of Cambridge, Massachusetts, whom I now introduce to you.

CENTENNIAL ADDRESS.

BY HON. JOEL PARKER, OF CAMBRIDGE, MASS.

FELLOW CITIZENS, FRIENDS; LADIES AND GENTLEMEN: — Some threescore years since, a favorite piece for declamation by the junior school-boys commenced with this couplet:

> " You 'd scarce expect one of my age.
> To speak in public on the stage."

When I received the invitation of the Committee of Arrangements, to deliver an Address, at the close of a century, more than three-quarters of which I represent, so far as years are concerned, in my own person, I was forcibly reminded of this school-boy exercise, and strongly tempted, reversing its significance, to make it the basis of my reply.

But the after-thought was, that upon such occasions, reminiscences are generally acceptable, even if they are trivial, and that, perhaps, urged by such a complimentary requisition, I owed it to the Town of my birth, to waive my claim to exemption, make my "last appearance" on this occasion, and tell what I know, little though it may be, of its early history.

Little enough it is, in fact, for the years of my early youth were passed in the remote seclusion of the Northeastern corner of the township, — and with only a few intervening years in the centre, my personal knowledge respecting its people, and its affairs, has been only through occasional visits.

If, " sixty years since" I had had even a remote suspicion, that I might stand here today, to discourse respecting the first inhabitancy of this town, and its incorporation, I would have come to you this morning with a portfolio full of notations respecting its ancient history.　Having no such premonition, many of the incidents of its early days have escaped from my grasp,—and the sources from which alone information respecting them could have been derived are gone forever.　The Century which is commemorated has, in the course of nature, carried away the Fathers who saw the inception of the settlement here, with those who immediately followed and were conversant with things done and transacted within its borders.

Even in regard to a much later date; a few only of that period seem to stand, somewhat like the servants of Job, who came from different quarters and said, one after another,—"I alone am escaped to tell thee;"—and doubtful upon whom I should charge the *duty* of having greater knowledge than I *ought* to have respecting the first half of the century, and thereby release myself from the conscription, by presenting a substitute, my conclusion, at last, led me, in obedience to the requisition, to come before you at the present time, and ask your indulgence for the deficiencies which you will perceive in what I have to offer for your acceptance.

The great antiquity of the Township where we are assembled does not admit of a doubt.

It seems to be the better opinion, that in the creation of the world, granite was first formed.　We are assured that granite appears to be the fundamental rock of the earth's crust, and that "wherever we reach the base of the stratified rocks, we find them resting upon granite."

This being so, it follows that New Hampshire is entitled to the credit of being part of the earliest creation.　And that Jaffrey had a larger interest in that creation than any of her neighbors, is shown by the fact, that on the subsequent partition, the larger portion of the Monadnock was assigned to her.

It is one of the jests about Father Sprague, as he was called, long the minister of Dublin, that discoursing one day upon faith, and quoting the passage of Scripture respecting its power to remove mountains, he turned his eye, through the window, to the mass of granite in full view, and expressed a doubt whether that applied to the Monadnock.

If there have been any very great changes in the structure of the earth here, since the period of creation, they are not chronicled. The Monadnock exhibits no evidence of disturbance, by faith, or by volcanic influences. The only fires have been upon its exterior surface. At the settlement of the Township it must have been covered, nearly to its summit, with a dense forest. Some of my earliest recollections are of fires on its sides, which furnished pillars of smoke by day, and of fire by night, sufficient to have guided the children of Israel, if their path to the promised land had lain in this vicinity. These fires left a tangled windfall, and a "bald rock," as it was called, at the top,—which was perhaps bare before that time. Possibly they are responsible, in some measure, for my inability to hunt up a respectable bear story, as a part of the minor history of the town.

But if the mountain has not changed its local habitation, the town has its geologic and historic problem, of a different character, in the meadow lying just east of this village. Some twenty years since, in one of my occasional visits to Jaffrey, I found Dr. Fox engaged in removing large pine stumps, with roots of great size and length, from his portion of the meadow, on the westerly side, and he showed me, at the distance of a rod or two from the upland, small pieces of wood bearing evidence of having been cut by the beavers, and supposed to be parts of a beaver dam, taken from a depth of some five feet below the surface. There were sticks of yellow birch and of alder about three or four inches in diameter, cut at the ends by a grooved instrument.

It was not surprising that the beavers should have had a habitation in that vicinity. In fact, recent inquiries show that this town must have been a favorite locality with them. But it was a mystery how, in the present conformation of the land, there could have been a beaver dam in that spot.

Recently it was determined to have a further examination, and it was soon ascertained that there had been a beaver dam at the outlet of the meadow, on the Southeast, near Mr. Cutter's tannery, — in the place which any sagacious beaver might have designated for a dam, — and the conclusion was readily reached, that what had been discovered by Dr. Fox was the remains of a beaver's cabin, on the Westerly shore of the pond which must have been formed by this dam. And so it proved. Selecting a spot a short distance from that opened by Dr. Fox, we struck another cabin, shown clearly to be such, by finding the beaver's bed, composed of small twigs, leaves and grass, well constructed in layers, — the general color being of a light orange when taken out, but becoming dark very soon, on exposure to the air. Many of the leaves were of perfect form, so that the kinds could be distinguished; and a small beech-nut was found between the sheets, probably not stowed away for use but taken up with the leaves in forming the bed.

All mystery about the formation of a beaver dam was solved, but there was a marvel remaining. The beaver's bed was about seven feet below the surface, and when made must have been in a dry position, and above the surface of a pond. By what process of accretion had this pond been filled, and some seven feet of mud deposited above the bed? On testing the depth of the mud with a pole, it was found to be about thirteen feet. In the centre of the meadow it must be much more.

The surrounding hills, at the present time, do not give evidence that great aid in filling could have been derived from them, — indicating that the basin must have filled itself, to a great extent, from its own resources. Sufficient material must perhaps have been washed in for the commencement of the process.

Dr. Fox states, that in clearing his meadow of these stumps and roots, he dug down into the mud in some places to the depth of ten feet; and that he found three tiers of large pine stumps, perhaps none directly over the others, but on three different levels, — one at the surface, the second about a foot below the bottom roots of the first, and the third about the same distance below the second, bringing the third about on the level with the beaver's cabin. — The trees were very large pines, generally three or four feet in diameter, and similar in the several tiers.

This statement is supplemented by Benjamin Cutter, Esq., who says, that in clearing his part of the meadow, he dug cross ditches, — and that at the intersection he found three large stumps in a perpendicular line, — the upper one directly above the other two, — the two upper of pines, one to two feet in diameter, — the lower apparently of birch and about one foot, — and that there were pine stumps at the surface, near, or quite, four feet in diameter, within, probably, ten rods.

That trees grow and decay is no marvel. But three successive generations of them, so to speak, situated on the same spot, and attaining this gigantic size, and on such a wet soil, formed to a great extent by their own decay, are not often seen or heard of, — never before to my knowledge.

Centuries seem to be comprised in this problem. Pine trees four feet in diameter do not grow in a short period, and when grown it requires some time to resolve them by a natural process of decay, into good meadow mud, capable of sustaining another like growth.

I can hardly assign less than five hundred years, perhaps it may be a thousand, — as a time when this beaver's cabin was erected and his bed made. How much longer, and how many tiers of pine trees there may have been below those discovered is not very material.

If any one is disposed to cavil about the exact period, I have no objection to discount a century or so ; but I cannot consent to give up any of the stumps, because as they stand, or rather stood, — the town may stump all the towns in the region round about, to show anything bigger, of that description.

It needs not that I should say to you, that it was persevering industry and diligent hard labor which subdued the forest here, and converted so large a portion of the township into reasonably fertile fields.

It must be admitted that the surface is somewhat uneven. — I should be unwilling to apply the term *rough* to the township, or to any body or thing connected with it. — And there are some stones scattered here and there, notwithstanding the " heaps of 'em " piled up in the fields, in times past, by the boys, somewhat to their disgust when they wanted to " go a fishing."

But this is a world of compensations.   Pure air, pure water, and good drainage, are conducive to good health, and good morals ; and it is but just to say, that this is a place where a man, under ordinary circumstances, may expect to " live out half his days," and even something more, if careful about his habits.

A party to ascend the Monadnock, after " haying time," was one of the recreations many years since ; — but who could then imagine, that our beloved Town, with its uneven surface, would become a celebrated resort for the seekers after health, and for the lovers of quiet and of the picturesque, and that the writers of prose, and eke of poetry, would come hither, not merely to get a larger view ef the world than they ever had before, but to make it a dwelling, and a habitation, and a shelter against the heats of summer, and perhaps the storms of adverse fortune.*

Respecting the minor incidents of the early history of the town, little can now be known, for the reasons suggested.

It is said that there were settlers here prior to seventeen hundred and forty-nine.   If so, they were occupants without even color of title, and doubtless did not remain.

If we desire to derive a title otherwise than from the original granite, we may trace it through the Right in the Crown of Great Britian by Discovery. — The grant of King James I, to the Council of Plymouth, in the County of Devon, in England. —The grant of that corporation to Capt. John Mason. — A devise by him to his grandson Robert Tufton, who took the name of Mason. — Thence as an entailed estate, through several descents to his great-grandson John Tufton Mason,—and after a recovery his conveyance in 1746, to Theodore Atkinson and

---

*I note, however, that the inducements to the traveller to "stop over," may not, within the law, be in all respects quite as numerous as those held out by a poetical landlord, who kept a tavern north of Keene village, some three-quarters of a century since.   They ran in this wise :
"Why will ye pass by, both hungry and dry,
Good brandy, good gin, please to walk in,
Good baiting, good bedding,
Your humble servant, Thomas Redding."

eleven other persons, who afterwards became known as "the Masonian Proprietors."

Acting under a vote of these Masonian Proprietors, passed June 16, 1749, Joseph Blanchard, of Dunstable, as their agent, on the thirtieth of November of that year, conveyed to Jonathan Hubbard and thirty-nine others, all the Right, Possession and Property of the Proprietors, to this township, then called the Middle Monadnock, or Number Two,—several of the grantees taking more than one share, the number of shares being in fact fifty.* The deed contained a provision by which the land should be divided into seventy-one shares, three shares being "granted and appropriated, free of all charge, one for the first settled minister," "one for the support of the ministry, and one for the school there forever,"† the grantors reserving for themselves eighteen shares, acquitted from all duty and charge until improved. And it was provided that each share contain three lots, equitably coupled together, and drawn for, at or before the first of July next, in some equitable manner.

One of the provisions of the deed was that each of the grantees should, at the executing of the instrument, pay twenty pounds old tenor, to defray the necessary charges arisen and arising in said township.‡

---

*See Appendix A.

†Grants of townships by the Governor and Council outside of the limits of the Masonian Proprietors, sometimes contained provisions giving shares to the Church of England, and to the Society for the propagation of the Gospel in Foreign Parts, with a large share for his Excellency personally.

‡The actual amount to be paid was but a small proportion of the nominal sum thus set down:—the old tenor being a paper currency issued long before by the Province, which, not having been redeemed according to its tenor, had greatly depreciated. Massachusetts had three emissions of paper currency, which became known as old tenor, middle tenor, and new tenor. The old tenor had depreciated in 1753, so that twenty shillings of it were worth only two shillings eight pence lawful money. It may be safely inferred that the currency of New Hampshire was not better. Probably it was worse. Belknap, speaking of a controversy between Governor Benning Wentworth and the Assembly, in 1749, respecting the representation of the towns, says:— "The effect of this controversy was injurious to the governor, as well as to the people. The public bills of credit had depreciated since this administration began, in the ratio of thirty to fifty-six, and the value of the governor's salary had declined in the same proportion."

There are conditions respecting clearing, building, and settlement, to be performed within certain specified times, by the several grantees, — a condition that a good convenient meeting-house should be built, as near the centre as might be with convenience, within six years from date, and ten acres of land reserved for public use: — another, that the grantees, or their assignees, by a major vote, in public meeting, should grant and assess such further sums as they should think necessary for carrying forward the settlement, — with a provision for the sale of so much of any delinquent's right as should be necessary for the payment of a tax, by a committee appointed for that purpose; — and a further provision that if any of the grantees should neglect or refuse to perform any of the articles, he should forfeit his share and right to those of the grantees who should have complied on their part, — with power to enter upon the right of the delinquent owner, and oust him, provided they should perform his duty as he should have done, within a year.

There were provisions by which the grantors undertook to defend the title, to a certain extent.

We are interested in these conditions and provisions only as matters of history, serving to show the measures taken by the Masonian Proprietors to secure the settlement of the townships which they granted, this among others.

It seems probable that none of the conditions were strictly complied with. They could not well be at that time. But so long as there were attempts, in good faith, to make settlements, it was not for the interest of the grantors to enforce forfeitures. Their shares became more valuable as the others were improved, and the enforcement of forfeitures, when there were attempts to perform, would have injured themselves.

I have procured from the Clerk of the Masonian Proprietors, copies of the documents on file in his office relating to this Township. A few items may perhaps be acceptable.

The grantees held a meeting at Dunstable, January 16, 1749-50, at which a vote was passed that each right be laid out into three lots, and to couple them fit for drawing, to be done by the last day of May; and that twenty pounds old tenor be raised to be raised to each right, to defray charges incidental thereto.

A plan of the township, seven miles long by five broad, laid out into ten ranges, and twenty-two lots one hundred rods wide to each range, was finished in May, 1750.

The meeting in January was adjourned to the first Tuesday in June, when it was again adjourned to the second Tuesday, at which time the lots were drawn.

It is probable that some of the grantees abandoned their rights, as six shares were sold at this meeting, and the money ordered to be deposited with the Treasurer, to be paid " to the first five men that goes on with their families in one year from this date, and continues there for the space of one year."

There was a vote also for a Committee to lay out a road from another Number Two (Wilton) through Peterboro' Slip, to this township.*

The meeting was then adjourned to November 8th, at which time a vote was passed prescribing the method of calling future meetings,—the provision for notice being the posting of notices at Dunstable, Lunenberg and Hollis. A further vote appointed Joseph Blanchard, Benjamin Bellows, and Captain Peter Powers, " a Committee to manage the Prudentials for this Society."

These last votes give us a clue to the residences of some of the grantees. They of course belonged to the towns where notices were to be posted. Captain Peter Powers, who was the grantee of four shares, and the purchaser of four of the six sold at auction at the first meeting,—and who was one of the Committee to manage the Prudentials,—must have been the first settler of Hollis, in 1731;—one of the soldiers under the celebrated Capt. John Lovewell, who fell in the Indian fight at Pigwackett, in 1725.

At a meeting of the grantees August 4, 1752, a formal vote was passed to accept the title with an acknowledgement that they

---

*Note.—Lyndeboro', including the Northerly part of Wilton, was laid out by Massachusetts under the claim of that Colony, and granted to certain persons, mostly belonging to Salem, in consideration of their sufferings in the expedition to Canada. The residue of what is Wilton was granted by the Masonian Proprietors, in 1749, and was called No. 2. Mason was called No. 1. Peterboro' Slip comprised the towns of Temple and Sharon. This gives us the general course of the road.

held it under the conditions, and limitations, and reservations; — by some of which there should have been clearings before that time.

Copies of the deed executed by Blanchard, and of the plan; and a list of the Proprietors, were filed in the office of the grantors September 4th, 1753.

It is stated that a settlement was attempted in 1753 by Richard Peabody, Moses Stickney and a few others, who remained but two or three years. The first native was a son of Moses Stickney, born in 1753.

The first permanent settlement was made in 1758, by John Grout and John Davidson.

There is in the files a paper containing, First, a list of settlers on the free lots to the number of nine families. Second, a list of settlers that abide constantly on settling rights, — total 22. Third, " some beginnings on settling rights," number 10. Also a memorandum, " no meeting-house built." This is certified as a true account of the settling rights " carefully examined and humbly submitted" by John Grout and Roger Gilmore. There is no date to it, nor any memorandum when it was received, but pinned to it is a paper signed John Gilmore and Roger Gilmore, dated March 10, 1769, addressed to " Gentlemen Grantors," setting forth, that they bought the right that was Paul March's, January, sixty-eight, and the improvements which they have made and intend, and concluding; " Gentlemen, we beg the favor of you, as you are men of honor, that you will not hurt us in our interest, for we have done everything in our power to bring forward the settlement of this place."

Roger Gilmore is the only one of the earlier settlers that I am sure of having seen. He lived on the hill east of the tannery of John Cutter, — was a man of large frame, and dignified deportment, — was highly esteemed, and was much employed as Justice of the Peace, Surveyor and in town offices and affairs.

There is also on file, " an accompt of the settlements in Monadnock No. 2," certified by Enoch Hale, stating the names of the settlers on the several rights, and the number of the rights, (ten in all), appearing to be delinquent. It is without date, but was " Received March 8th, 1770," and was probably made up within a short time previously. From this it appears that there were settlements on thirty-four rights; and twelve lots (additional as I understand,) improved; — and that mills were erected on Right 15, and a saw-mill on 41.

And here, near the close of its unincorporated existence, let us pay a deserved tribute to the enterprise and energy of the early settlers.

Struggling against obstacles that were all but insuperable, and through hardships which might well have daunted the most determined courage, they have, in a few years, brought the township largely above the average of the settlements in the County, and to a position exceeded only by towns of a longer existence, all of which had much greater facilities for access.

The particular obstacles which they encountered, and the details of the hardships which they endured, we cannot know. Of their personal deprivations and sufferings, we fail to form an adequate conception. It is difficult to gain even a general appreciation of them.

There are, it is true, only forty miles intervening between the head-quarters, if we may so call them, at Dunstable, but twenty or more of them are through a nearly trackless, dense forest, over a rough, rocky surface, with occasionally a small natural meadow.

The pioneers make their slow, painful way, much of it through the thick under-brush, — the husband with an axe on his shoulder, and what he can carry of household appendages in a pack on his back, and his wife follows, somewhat similarly loaded, except the axe. Cheap land, within the reach of their scanty means, has tempted them to endurance. There may be a young man with them. God be thanked we do not see any young children. Weary, worn in spirit, as well as in body, they reach the range and lot of their destination, and their first shelter is constructed of hemlock boughs, with the same material for a bedstead, and leaves for a mattress.

A rude log hut follows.* And then comes the hard struggle with the forest, and with privation, — with the winter, its deep snows, and its intense cold. There is no communication with the outward world but by " rackets," (snow-shoes), and pioneers of longer duration are in other towns, miles away. It is not necessary to put wild beasts into this picture.

Is it wonderful that the settlers of '53 found this too great an endurance, even for their brave hearts, and strong arms, and that they abandoned the settlement, when remaining threatened their lives? Or rather is it not wonderful that they lived to abandon it? Surely it was not light difficulties which would deter persons who had the courage to begin such a work, from the prosecution of their purpose.

But there is another attempt at settlement made under more favorable auspices.

We may suppose that the few pounds voted to be raised to make a road from No. 2 have been expended. The underbrush and some of the stones are cleared away, and trees are blazed along the route; and another small party of settlers start, with oxen, not in yokes, but single file, with such loads as they can carry strapped upon their backs. And there is a cow there. The small patches of natural meadow furnish food for the animals, and the emigrants arrive with better means of establishing themselves. — The trees fall, — the logs are drawn, piled, burnt, — a small space is cleared, — a shelter is built, — seed is sown, and the vegetation, anxiously watched and tended, gives a scanty crop. But sickness comes. Exposure has produced its natural result; — fever is in the household. There is no physician. The medicines are the few simple remedies brought in the luggage. Acts of neighborly kindness would be cheerfully rend-

---

*The log hut must have been an institution of short duration. So far as I have heard, there is little tradition of log-houses in the town. A grist and saw mill were erected in Peterboro' as early as 1751. Another saw mill near the place of the South Factory, in 1758. Rev. John H. Morison, in his very interesting Address at the Centennial Celebration in Peterboro', says : " at this period [1770] log huts were little used. Substantial frame houses, many of them two stories high, had been erected." And we have seen, from the return of 1770, that there were then two saw mills here.

ered, if there were near neighbors, but are of difficult procurement in this forest of " magnificent distances," and all the hours of attendance by the sick bed are so much time withdrawn from what would otherwise have been essentially necessary for labor and for rest. — Alas! the kindest care, the unslumbering watch, and the fervent prayer, are unavailing, and the sufferer, no longer such, is laid to final rest in some quiet corner of " the clearing."

Out of this darkness comes a brighter dawn. Lumber can be had. The mills are miles distant, to be sure, and the transportation difficult, but perseverance overcomes obstacles. " The road " has been improved. — There is a horse upon the path. — The rider has a young child in her lap, and one somewhat older sits behind. — Her husband drives " the stock." The way is not so toilsome, — there are more articles of housekeeping in the luggage, — more of encouragement, more of hope, more of fruition, more of happiness.

We have reached 1770, and there are several families here. The settlement is established on a firm basis.

Let us never fail to do justice to the pioneers, men and women, who with such resolute courage, fortitude, patience and perseverance, established a civilized society in the midst of a trackless wilderness.

We should do ourselves a great wrong, if we did not express our deep admiration of them.

In 1771, the Province was divided into Counties. Prior to this time all the public offices were in Portsmouth or the vicinity, and the Courts were held there.

In an Act for making a new proportion of public taxes, passed May 28, 1773, which included unincorporated places, Monadnock No. 2 is set down at £3–5s in the £1000. The proportion for Cheshire County, which until 1827, included what is now Sullivan County, was £117–8s. There were twelve towns in the County rated higher than Jaffrey, and seventeen towns and places at less. This proportion of the taxation serves to show, in some measure, its relative importance, at that time.

The Masonian Proprietors had and claimed only a right of property. Their title to the land passed by the deed authorized by them, as a deed passes the title to land at the present day; but there was no right of town government granted. The provision for taxing the shares, and collecting the tax, could only be made effectual through the laws of the Province. The jurisdiction was in the Governor and Council, and the Assembly.

The grantees of the lands acted like a corporation for the division and disposition of their lands, and the performance of their duties as a Proprietary, but for nothing beyond. When those things were accomplished, the Proprietary was at an end, — dissolved. And this was true also of the townships granted by the Governor, outside of the limits of the Masonian lines, unless incorporated.

There was no provision in the general laws by which an assessment could be made upon the inhabitants of unincorporated places, for which reason the Act apportioning the public taxes, in 1773, contained a provision appointing persons, who were named, to call meetings of the inhabitants of such places, and requiring the inhabitants at such meetings to choose the necessary officers for assessing and collecting the tax, and giving authority for that purpose.

And so the time had come when the interests of the people required corporate powers, of a general character, and on the 17th of August, 1773, an Act of Incorporation was granted, nominally by His Majesty, George III, but in fact by the Royal Governor, John Wentworth, with advice of the Council, — the corporate name being found in the name of one of the Masonian Proprietors, who was then Secretary; and *Jaffrey* was installed into the great brotherhood of political and municipal incorporations, called Towns; which have been of such incalculable benefit not only to New England, where they originated, and of which they are the glory and the pride, but through it to the country at large.

The centuries of which we usually speak, date from the commencement of the christian era, — occasionally from the period assigned by Biblical Theology as the time of the creation of the world.

But a century may have its beginning at any point of time. That of which we now witness the close had its inception with this incorporation. If the event be supposed to be one of comparative insignificance, it was one which has had a greater absolute force, for the promotion of the happiness of those persons inhabiting within the limits of the town, than any of the greater ones which have astonished the world.

If we should suspend, for a moment, the consideration of the local interests attached to this incorporation, and which entitle it to mark the commencement of a century, and its anniversary to a grateful recognition and celebration, and should turn our attention to the general history of the century which has followed, we should find that this century may challenge a comparison with any one which has preceded it, whatever date may be assigned for the commencement of the latter.

But we must not undertake the centennial history of the world to-day. On our recollection of it, however, we may surely be pardoned if we exclaim,— Great has been the century which had its commencement in the incorporation of the town of Jaffrey!

These incorporated towns had their origin in Plymouth, Duxbury, and Scituate, in the Plymouth Colony,— followed by Charlestown, Salem and Newton, (since Cambridge,) and Dorchester, in Massachusetts,— and by Portsmouth, Dover, Exeter, and Hampton, in this state.

It has been suggested that the Town Organization had its origin in the Congregational Church polity,— and in fact the organization of the church, in the earlier settlements of the Pilgrims and the Puritans, accompanied the organization of the town.

But the town grew mainly out of the secular need,—out of the democratic principle of self-government,—as is shown from the fact that changes in the modes and forms of worship, and in the different church organizations, have not affected the Townships, and the Towns;—Whereas Congregationalism had no existence outside of the portions of the country where these Townships existed. Instead of creating Townships and Towns, it has not itself been created to any extent, where they have not existed. It cannot well exist without them. But they now exist in the Western country, where Congregationalism has as yet little foothold,— and but for them it would have been long since merged in Presbyterianism, which has been the prevailing form of orthodoxy in all parts of the country where these towns have been unknown.*

Considering the principles and objects of the emigrants, the town system may be said to have been a necessity, in the existing state of things, in the early settlement of this part of the country. It was the only organization by and through which the settlers could best provide for their wants, and have the full enjoyment of the liberty which they prized so highly;—and they devised it accordingly.

The early settlers of the Plymouth Colony discovered, that the grant of corporate powers to the small separate settlements, and the passage of general laws giving them such powers and privileges as would enable them to provide for their local needs, and subjecting them to the performance of such duties as might be required by the government of the whole Colony, was the best and fittest way for the transaction of the affairs of the different localities, and they so provided. — This conclusion was reached, not through any revelation which perfected the system at once, but by degrees, through their daily and yearly experience; and the system, inaugurated at Plymouth, commended itself to the Massachusetts Colony, so that it was adopted there at the outset.

The earliest settlements in this State were commenced in a slightly different manner, Portsmouth, Dover, and Hampton being towns, independent of each other, with separate powers of government, exercised by agreement, without any act of Incorporation. But when the government of the Colony of New Hampshire was organized, grants of townships were made and towns incorporated.

In this organization of towns, the settlements of New England differed from those of Virginia, and other Southern States,

*See Appendix B.

and to these towns, providing for local wants, and performing local duties, New England owes much of the prosperity, of which she has had a reasonable share to this day.

The early settlers in this place, like those of other towns, wanted religious teachers and institutions. This is shown, not merely by the character of mankind, the nature of society, and the particular character of the parties, but by the provisions in the grant of the township giving one share for the first settled Minister, and one for the support of the Ministry, and by the condition requiring that a good convenient meeting-house should be built near the centre within six years.

Whatever we may think respecting ourselves, at this later day, with our more dense population, and our enlarged means, we may well conclude, that at that period, it was for the benefit of the civil state, that the institutions of religion should be maintained through some organization having legal power to provide for the support of religious teachers. In fact the authority of the towns to provide for the settlement of ministers and their support, remained until 1819, although the efficiency of the law was much impaired, by religious divisions, at an earlier day. The clergyman had then no need to spend his summer in Europe, or the Adirondacks. His parish being the town, — his parochial visits furnished him with sufficient " muscular christianity " for all practical purposes.

They wanted schools, and of course they needed school-houses, — and for the erection of these, school districts. The inhabitants of the town, with a full understanding of the local needs of all portions of the town, could arrange these districts, — the people of the several districts could then determine the situation and the size of the house required, with regard to their accommodation, and pecuniary ability ; — and the tax voted by the town for the support of schools, being divided in an equitable manner, could then be applied to the purposes of education, in these districts with the greatest possible efficiency. — The poor little school houses would not make a great show by the side of some modern structures, — but they did a work, perhaps quite as useful as if the seats had had cushions, and the desks had been of mahogany.

They wanted highways. This need of facilities for intercommunication, and for intercourse with other portions of the country, must have impressed itself upon them, by the inconvenien-
ces which they suffered, in a manner to assure an energetic use
of their powers in this respect, — and the town incorporation,
with its power to divide into districts for this purpose, and by
the appropriation of money or labor, to be expended under
surveyors interested to do a good work, soon rendered travel
safe, and even convenient. The great rocks have disappeared,
one after another, under the persevering application of the highway tax, until the "drives" have, as you know, become very attractive.

The then existing modes of travel and transportation did not
require roads of the most perfect construction. Chaises had not
been introduced. The light Dearborn wagon had not been invented. The single horse had no difficulty in picking his way,
and by skilful "hawing and geeing," the oxen and cart were
enabled to avoid the more formidable obstructions. Personal
transportation was mostly on horseback ; but the cart was made
the carryall when several persons were to be conveyed. The
side-saddle furnished a healthful means of locomotion for the
women, and when it became necessary to ride double, the pillion, no longer known alas, formed a very comfortable seat for
the lady. As it was necessary in order to keep the seat properly, that she should pass her arm around the side of the gentleman, this was, in some cases, a very acceptable mode of transportation to the junior portion of the community.

No system of general legislation could provide for all these
local wants and necessities, according to the exigencies of particular cases.

But the general laws enabled these small communities, acting
as municipal corporations, to provide each for itself, in relation
to these and other matters, according to its own views of what
it needed, and what it could perform ; it being premised that it
had needs upon some subjects, to some extent, and *must* perform
to that extent, at least,—with liberty to do more, which it usually
did.— Thus it must raise a certain amount of money for the sup-

port of schools,— and might raise more if deemed expedient.

The powers and privileges which the towns possessed were not talents to be wrapped in a napkin, and buried in the earth, nor did the people belong the class of slothful and unfaithful servants who seek to escape from their duties.

There were other duties and rights attached to these incorporations. The duty of supplying the needs of the aged, and infirm, and incompetent, who were unable to supply themselves; so that want and destitution should be alleviated, and starvation unknown, was deemed a common duty of each community,— and could best be performed by these incorporations.

Through them, also, the inhabitants were primarily to enjoy such political rights as were conceded to the people in the days of the Province, and the more extended and exalted powers which were conferred by the acquisition of Independence, the organization of the State, and the adoption of the Constitution of the United States.— All the rights of suffrage were to be exercised within the town incorporation, the electors being summoned thereto by its warrants for such purposes.— Again,— the meetings held for these purposes gave opportunity for the full consideration and discussion of the measures required for the public good, and for the expression of the opinions of the inhabitants respecting them. How many of the specifications of the Declaration of Independence originated in the Resolutions of the towns we cannot now know.— Although no trace may be left, we know that there must have been arguments for and against the adoption of the Constitution of the United States, when the Delegates were chosen to attend the Convention which ratified it by a small majority, proposing divers amendments,— most of which were adopted immediately afterwards. Some voted against the ratification, fearing that such amendments would not be made,— perhaps so instructed by their constituents.

Nothing could have been better adapted to the execution of all these purposes than these "little Democracies," as De Tocqueville has called them.

The social privileges connected with the organization must not be overlooked. It made the inhabitants of the small tract of terri-

tory within its limits. a brotherhood.— promoting the welfare of
each other and of the whole community. by the meeting-house,
the school-house, and the highway,— and in these, and other
ways, establishing good order, social intercourse, and a kindly
feeling towards each other.

The Town was the efficient means which secured the prosperity of the household.   The several families, farmers, mechanics,
laborers, and professional persons. needed, for the development
of their resources. and the greatest enjoyment of their privileges,
something beyond their isolated households. — something beyond
even the mutual support of each other in their various neighbor-
hoods, and they found it in the Town.   It enlarged, while it
concentrated. their sympathies, formed and moulded their opinions, and gave expression to their united will.   Lastly, the mil-
itary company organizations were mostly within the Town, —
two Communities sometimes uniting to furnish an extra article
in this line.   From these companies the ranks of the army have
been recruited in time of war,—being liable to draft if necessary.

In the time of the Revolution, when the ordinary mode of
supplying the army seemed likely to fail, requsitions were made
upon the towns to furnish ammunition and provisions, and were
promptly answered.   They were often the storehouses of ammunition.

If any one who does not know, wou'd seek an exemplification
of the utility of the Town incorporations, let him look at Jaffrey
today, and study her history.

An admirable result of the Town organization was, that the
Revolution, which followed almost immediately upon the incorporation of this Town, did not place the country in a state of
disintegration.   The Town organization remained, — its efficiency necessarily somewhat impaired,— but the town officers, having
been elected by the people, still retained their confidence and
support.   Such powers as could be exercised only in the name
of the king, or under the royal authority, were at first suspended, and then abrogated ; but the same powers were immediately
exercised under the authority of the people ; and the towns during all the time served to a great extent the purposes for which
they were established.

A Revolutionary Convention, called by the Committee of Correspondence, in 1775, recommended that those who had been chosen into office in the usual manner should, as formerly, be considered the proper officers, and that the town, selectmen and other officers proceed in the usual manner in granting and collecting monies, &c., unless some particular direction was given ; —adding this significant paragraph :—

" If any, inimical to their country, or inattentive to the ruin which must ensue upon a contrary conduct, should refuse, we trust that all the friends of the country will effectually strengthen the hands of the selectmen, constables and collectors."

It is not supposed that any one here by his refusal rendered it necessary, even to hint at a resort to the peculiar strengthening plaster, thus indicated.

February 13, 1775, the town voted unanimously to visit Mr. Williams, of Keene,—a very extraordinary civility on the face of the vote. Williams was a lawyer, but the call on him was not for professional advice. — He was a tory, and this unusual demonstration had reference to that fact. The further proceedings in relation to the proposed visit are not of record. — It is a fair presumption that there was no tory in Jaffrey who might be visited with much less trouble.

No other system could so well have supplied civil government, under such circumstances.

It was more difficult to deal with matters of which the Courts of Justice had jurisdiction. The Courts, on recommendation of the Convention, adjourned.

Justices of the Peace could not well issue compulsory process under the royal authority, in the existing circumstances. The collection of debts by suit was suspended, and the natural consequences were, in one instance at least, exemplified here. In the files of the Convention of 1775, is a memorial, or representation, address to the " Honorable Provincial Congress " signed by Jethro Bailey, William Turner and Roger Gilmore, Committee of Correspondence, setting forth that Benjamin Nutting of Peterboro' Slip, so called, had entered a complaint to them against John Davis, Junior, of Jaffrey, that upon the second day of October, instant, as he came to the house of John Eaton, on some business, he was assaulted by said Davis, and abused in the most "solem" manner, as appears by sundry evidences,—that notwithstanding Davis was notified to attend and hear the evidences examined, he refused, — that he had often been requested to settle the matter, but remained obstinate, and persisted in his villainy, with insolence.

The Committee enclosed the depositions and earnestly desired the Convention to take the matter into consideration, and either determine it between them, or invest the Committee with a proper authority to act, with instructions how to proceed in the case. It does not appear that any action was taken upon the subject.

On the fifth of January, 1776, a " Form or Plan of Civil Government" was adopted by a Convention, or Congress, which met for the purpose, under which the affairs of the towns were again transacted in legal form. The Form of Government was limited by its terms to continue " during the present unhappy contest with Great Britian," but served as a State Constitution for many years, and has been said to be the first State Constitution. But this is a mistake, North Carolina having formed one a few days earlier.

This caused no change in the organization of the Town, or in its proceedings, except that the latter were now conducted, once more, under what proved to be a sufficient legal authority.

A few items in relation to the increase of the population, and the rate of taxation, may serve to show the comparative progress with the other towns.

The Convention of 1775, ordered a survey to be made of the people in the several counties, for the purpose of determining the ratio of representation in the Assembly, from which it appears that Jaffrey had 351 inhabitants. Of thirty towns in the County, ten or eleven had a larger number. She had sixteen men in the army. This is a very strong delegation for such a small community, just organized, — larger than any of the towns not having more inhabitants. Keene had 756 inhabitants. Chesterfield, Westmoreland and Richmond a still greater number.

The Census, in 1790, gives Jaffrey a population of 1235. There were then only six towns in the County with a population greater than this, and these, with the exception of Keene, lay on the South border, or on the Connecticut River, and so were more easy of access. Keene had 1314 inhabitants.

In 1800 the population was 1341. Eleven towns had a larger population, mostly much more favorably situated. Keene had 1645.

By an Act of the Assembly in 1777, determining the proportion of each town for every £1000 of the State taxes, Jaffrey's proportion was £5–9s.–5d. There were nine towns in the County having a greater valuation, — that of Keene being £10–5s.–9d., — twenty-two having less.

When, in 1780, a requisition was made for a hundred and twelve thousand weight of beef for the army, the proportion of Jaffrey was 7326 pounds; the proportion of Keene 11,309. The same year a new proportion of taxes gave Jaffrey £6–10s.–10d., Keene £10–1s.–11d.

Another proportion in 1789 shows a comparative increase, favorable to the prosperity of Jaffrey,—that is, supposing that the duty to pay a larger proportion of taxes indicates in fact a larger ability to perform the duty, — which probably is not always the case. Jaffrey is set at £7–12s.–5d., Keene £9–19s.–6d.

Another proportion in 1794 gave for Jaffrey £7–9s.–8d., Keene £9–14s.–6d. But in this year the valuation of Chesterfield, Walpole and Westmoreland, lying on the Connecticut River, each exceeded that of Keene.

It is not my purpose to refer in detail to the proceedings of the town, in the exercise of its rights and the performance of its duties. This is the special province of the future historian, and to him, whoever he may be, I remit it.

But a few brief notes, having reference to some of the subjects which have been mentioned, may find a place upon this occasion. The first meeting under the act of incorporation was for the choice of town officers only. It was called by Jonathan Stanley, specially authorized by the Charter, August 27, 1773, and was held September 14.

Another meeting was held September 28, to raise money for the building of roads, and the support of the Gospel.

April 26, 1774, it was voted to build a meeting-house; and July 6, to build one of larger dimensions, — to let the building at public vendue, — that it should be raised by the middle of June next, at the town's cost, — with several other votes on the subject.

It was voted in March 1775, that the Committee to build, provide all things necessary to raise the house at the cost of the town. But March 30, 1780, there was a vote to make allowance to Captain Henry Coffin for the barrel of rum which he paid for, to raise the meeting-house. The Captain it would seem, intervened patriotically, to supplement the deficiency of the provision made by the Committee, and waited a long time for reimbursement.

There is a tradition that the meeting-house was raised on the day of the battle of Bunker Hill, and that the guns of that battle were heard here. But this must be a mistake. When the matter is examined, the probabilities are against it. It is hardly probable that guns fired at Charlestown could be heard here, with the New Ipswich hills and the forest intervening, even on a quiet day, when there was no meeting-house to raise. Moreover, the battle was on Saturday, which was as good a day for a battle as any other day, but would hardly be selected as the time to raise a meeting-house, lest there should be some work remaining which ought to be performed the next day.

The conclusion to be derived from the improbabilities is fortified by direct hear say evidence. I received a letter a few days since from Dr. Jeremiah Spofford, of Groveland, Mass., in which he says, " My father, Jeremiah Spofford, as a master carpenter, framed that church. He was employed to do it by Captain Samuel Adams, whose wife was his sister. Jacob Spofford and Joseph Haskell went up with him, to work on the frame. * * * My father often related, seventy years ago, that they raised the house, and that ending his job, they set out for home the next day, travelling " *ride and tie*," three men, with one horse to carry tools and ease the men in turn; — that coming down through

Townsend, in the forenoon, they heard the roar of cannon, which proved to be the cannon of Bunker Hill, and coming over the Westford Hills, in the evening, they saw the light of Charles-town burning. * * * * * Captain Adams was one of the contractors to build the house, and was a carpenter himself."

It may be objected that "unlucky" Friday, was as little like-ly as Saturday to be selected as the day to begin such a work. But the explanation seems easy. The town had voted to raise by the middle of June. The contract would naturally specify that as the time of performance. There would be a desire, and time enough, for compliance. The fifteenth of June was Thurs-day. If we suppose that to be the day selected, and that there was some unfinished work to be done on Friday, to complete the job, we shall have the carpenters on their homeward way on Saturday, in the localities in which Mr. Jeremiah Spofford placed them.

We may give up the tradition without a sigh. Neither the meeting-house, nor the battle will suffer by the loss of it.

There was some delay in settling a minister. Several candi-dates were hired. There was a vote that young men supply the pulpit; and some others indicating that the services of some of the candidates were not quite satisfactory. But June 1st, 1780, it was voted to hear Mr. Caleb Jewett more, if he can be ob-tained; and September 4th, a vote to concur with the church in giving him a call. Why he did not accept, does not appear.— Perhaps from the insufficiency of the salary offered. He was, I think, a graduate of Dartmouth, of 1776, a native of Newbury, Mass., and afterwards settled in Gorham, Maine.

In 1782, they settled the Rev. Laban Ainsworth, a native of Woodstock, Connecticut;—a graduate of Dartmouth College in 1778.

The first vote for a salary was for £70 " while he supplies the desk,"—which was afterwards changed to " while he remains the minister of the town." Choosing with deliberation, they are en-titled to the credit of having abided by their determination.— Mr. Ainsworth lived to the age of more than a hundred years, —officiated without a colleague until 1832,—and remained as

the pastor of the church until his death, but his labors were dis-
continued a few years earlier.   As many of you knew him well,
I need not speak of his appearance or services.   A withered
right arm was probably the reason why he did not write his sermons.   If, as has been said, he sometimes looked up his text on
Sunday morning, after breakfast, the fact will serve to show his
confidence in his powers of discussion.

The tales respecting the jokes, practical and otherwise, passing between him and Father Sprague, are numerous, many of
them probably fictitious.   But there was, unquestionably, a sufficient encounter of wits to lay a good foundation for some of
them.

In the infancy of such a settlement, the difficulties of establishing and maintaining a school or schools would necessarily be
very great.   If the means of support had been abundant, the
facilities for the attendance of the scholars must have been quite
limited.

The first appropriation of £8 was made April 13, 1775.

Soon we find votes for the division of the money, indicating
schools in different parts of the township, — then a division into districts.

That the interests of education have received full support
here, may be inferred from the fact, that twenty-four young men
have graduated at the different colleges.   Twenty of them at
Dartmouth.

It is not surprising that they deemed expenditures upon the
roads as of the first importance. — Will you think it strange
when I say that they appropriated much larger sums for highways than they did for the support of the gospel and the schools ?
Will you be astonished that at their second meeting they voted
£80, lawful money, to be worked out on the roads, and only £6
to procure preaching, and that this disparity increased so that
April 13, 1775, when they voted £8 for the school, they again
voted £6 for preaching, and £130 for the roads ?

We must recollect that the efficiency of their maintenance of
preaching depended upon their first mending their ways.

It may be said, that roads lay at the foundation of their prosperity, spiritual, as well as temporal.   Without roads the settlement could not succeed; and if that failed, the support of religious teaching, and the school failed with it.   As the roads were
made better, settlements were encouraged, the ability to support
the institutions of religion was enlarged, and the appropriations
were enlarged also.

It is with great regret that I refer again to my inability to give
some better account respecting the earliest inhabitants.

Perhaps my recollections of a later date may possess some interest, and serve with those of others, to fill a page of local history.

In the early part of the present Christian century, there was
clustered in the vicinity of the meeting-house, which then had
no steeple, the house of Rev. Mr. Ainsworth at the Southeast
corner of the Common,—Danforth's Tavern, where Cutter's Hotel now stands,—the store of Joseph Thorndike, Esq., and David Page's store, on the East side, Cragin's Saddlery Shop on
the Northeast corner, and on the North a large pile of buildings
belonging to Joseph Cutter, Esq., of which only the main dwelling-house now remains.   He kept a tavern, and had very ample
accommodations for his customers.   He was, I think, much the
largest landholder in the township, and had an ambition to settle each of his numerous sons on a farm, which he accomplished
to a great extent.   At the Southwest corner of the burying
ground was a school-house.   East of Danforth's Tavern was his
blacksmith's shop, North of which was the dwelling-house of
Capt. Samuel Adams.

Commencing at the Common, the road to the Northeast, leading to Peterboro', and to the Southeasterly part of Dublin, passed
by a small house on the corner, at the left, no longer there,—
which was occupied at one time by Mr. Cummings, afterwards
by Dr. Johnson, and by Jonathan Lufkin,—there turning North
the road extended, by the place where the Melville Academy
now stands, less than a quarter of a mile, where it forked, the direct road proceeding Northerly towards Dublin, by the houses
of Mr. Newton and Thomas French, —the Easterly fork, which

was the principal road, running over the hill by a house occupied by David Smiley, Esq., Attorney at Law.

This house has gone, and the road over the hill has gone with it. The more modern route, Northeast, by Mr. John Cutter's tannery, and Easterly of the meadow, entered this old road at the foot of the hill, on the East.

Nearly a mile East of the village was the house of Widow Bryant.

The road forked a few rods Easterly. On the Northerly branch, which branched again, lived Samuel Cary, Benjamin Lawrence, Deacon Jesse Maynard, Azael Gowing, Moses Stickney, Samuel Stickney, Silas Pierce, Jacob Jewell, Benj. Frost.

Proceeding a short distance, the Easterly branch appeared to run into a North and South road, but the Northerly part was the main road to the Northeast. A few rods to the South was the house of Alpheus Crosby. In front, that of Asa Sawyer.

Pursuing the main road, at a distance of about half a mile, on the right side, — was the house of Lieut. Thomas Adams, which has disappeared. Another was built near, on the left side, many years since, occupied by Daniel Emery. Not far beyond, at the place where a road now leads off to the East village, there came into this road from the West a short branch road on which lived Mr. Bates. At this point came another fork. On the Northerly branch which has been slightly changed at its commencement, a quarter of a mile brought the traveller to another fork, the Westerly road being merely a local branch, terminating at the house soon after owned by Samuel Pierce. On the Easterly or main branch, we came next to the school-house of the district of my early boyhood,—and in the field some quarter of a mile Southeast was the house of Ebenezer Burpee.

Miss Hitty Brooks was one of the teachers of the summer school, a most estimable young lady, whose kindness dwells in my memory. She afterwards married Samuel Pierce.

The old school-house has disappeared, and a few years more will carry all its memories with it. A few of its inmates at a later date still remain.

Starting once more upon our way, we find next where was the house of Whitcomb Powers, at the base of the hill, on the left. It is no longer there. There was none a little onward, where the residence of my late friend Levi Fisk, Esq., has stood for many years. On the Northerly branch of a fork of the road a few rods further running to Twitchell's mills, in the Easterly part of Dublin, was the house of his father Thomas Fisk. At the fork last mentioned was formerly the shop of John Pushee, of which nothing but the ruins remained so far back as I can recollect. I have the impression it had been burned.

Thence, pursuing the Easterly branch of the highway, next came the house of my father, who came here from Pepperell in May, 1780, settled in the unbroken forest, and cleared his farm himself, with such assistance as he could obtain. Some of you know the place. I am not aware of the particular inducement which led him to settle there. Probably a representation that it was a nice bit of land, dog cheap; — and cheapness was a consideration not to be despised.* It proved rough and rocky, and admitted of any amount of hard labor. Twenty-five years of patient, persevering industry had made a difference in the appearance of things. There were rods of stone wall, requiring some knowledge of the mysteries of compound addition, to say how many. There were cattle and sheep, — hay in the barn,— a patch of flax in the field; — and a little wheel, and a great wheel, and a great loom in the house.† The wood pile, would have deemed itself neglected if it had not extended a hundred feet, "more and not less," along the wall, with an indefinite breadth, and a height which no one undertook to measure. The fire-place in the common working-room, received back logs two and a half feet in diameter. I am tempted to put on the other half foot, but refrain. From the great brick oven, by the side of fire place, there issued, from time to time, baked pump-

---

*Consideration 260 pounds, lawful money, — 102 acres of land, part of lot 20 in the first range.
†Girls "hired themselves out" to spin. When the cloth was fulled and dressed, the tailoress of the neighborhood came, cut, and made up the clothes. — When the hides were tanned, the shoemaker, in his rounds, came once or twice in the year, and made up a stock of boots and shoes for the family, staying perhaps a week for the purpose.

kins, such as no cooking stove, invented or to be invented, can ever produce, — and there was no watering of the milk.

On winter evenings apples were roasting and sputtering upon the hearth, — and there was a mug of cider there. Checkers and jack-straws were seen occasionally, and some card teeth were set.

My brothers caught minks, and musquash, partridges and pickerel, rabbits and woodchucks, — and in haying time, I took up bumble bees' nests, getting poor pay for my labor.

In order to economise time, I give this brief sketch of a single household, instead of a more elaborate statement which I was preparing respecting farming life generally in the town ; — and in the hope that the personality may be excused, in consideration of its brevity. Any one by pursuing things to their natural antecedents and conclusions, may judge somewhat of the whole from these few particulars. Exceptions of course.*

Half a mile onward was the house of the Widow Turner.— The widow relished a joke, and perhaps I may be pardoned for telling a short story, which she told herself. She had taken her grist to be ground at the mills of Samuel Twitchell, Esq., the father of the celebrated surgeon Dr. Amos Twitchell, just within the limits of Dublin, riding, of course, upon the top of the bags. The Squire who was somewhat of a humorist, had a hired man named White, certainly not beautiful to behold. The widow's description of what occurred further was in this wise :—

" When I got there the Squire was in the yard, and I said to him, ' help me off my horse, Squire ; ' which he did. Then I said to him, ' now kiss me Squire; ' and he turned and called ' White, White, White; ' as if he was calling some great dog, and there came out of the mill the ugliest looking critter that ever I set

---

*The manufactures of cotton were those of the household, operated by hand power. Edmund Snow, of Peterboro', manufactured hand cards for cotton and wool, punching the holes in the leathers, and preparing the teeth and distributing them among the different families in the region round about. to be set by the young people, who in that way put " store pay " in their purse. At the Peterboro' Centennial in 1839, my brother Isaac gave some account of his achievements in setting these card teeth. Perhaps it was in this way that he was led to take an interest in the establishment of cotton manufacturies in Peterboro' and elsewhere.

my eyes on, and the Squire said, 'Come here, White, and kiss this woman ;—I always keep a man to do that drudgery for me.' "

A short distance farther, at the extreme Northeast corner of the town, was Samuel Saunders, a very good carpenter as well as a farmer. Here the road turned short to the South, and passing the house of Elijah Wellman, connected near the line oi Peterboro' with the Southerly branch, which was left soon after passing Lieut. Adams's. A house has existed South of Wellman's, occupied by Andrew Holmes, but I think of a later date.

Turning back to the Southerly branch, and taking the direction to Peterboro', there was near the fork the house of Roger Brigham. Then came the house of David Sawtell, then Parker Maynard, then Samuel Patrick, then Mr. Snow.

Samuel Dakin, Esq., Attorney at Law, who afterwards removed to New Hartford, in the State of New York, purchased land North of Capt. Adams, in the middle of the town, and built the house now occupied by Dr. Fox, about 1805. My father, having bought a corner lot of Mr. Dakin, erected the house at the Northerly end of that street, and I became an inmate of the school-house at the corner of the burying ground. There is a reminiscence of discipline connected with this house. The rules of the school forbid whispering of course. Having a desire to say something to a young Miss who sat near me, I forgot the rule I suppose, and she must have joined in the transgression, for the eagle eye of the teacher, Miss Maria Blanchard, detecting this violation of order, we were forthwith sentenced to sit each with an arm around the other's neck. I do not give this as an instance of the ordinary discipline. On the contrary it was an unusual, as well as a cruel punishment, and may therefore be regarded as unconstitutional. But to prevent misapprehension, I have taken occasion to say, that I have since seen the time when I should have borne such a dispensation with a much greater degree of philosophy.*

---

*The school books were Webster's Spelling Book, with a grim frontispiece, supposed to represent that ambitious lexicographer, Webster's Third Part, American Preceptor, The Columbian Orator, Young Ladies' Accidence, Murray's Grammar, Morse's Geography, and Pike's Arithmetic.

Pursuing the road Northwesterly from the school-house, there was at the foot of the hill, a house occupied by Widow Hale, then one occupied by Hugh Gragg, and a few rods Westerly, at the junction of the old road running Westerly to Marlboro' and the road running Northerly to Dublin, there was in the corner, the house of Dr. Adonijah Howe the elder, the beloved physieian. He afterwards built a much larger one just North, which you have known as occupied by Daniel Cutter. The place is now designated as the Shattuck Farm. Jonathan Gage lived off Northeast from this point, on a private road. A house has since been built, farther on the Dublin road, by Joel Cutter, and beyond this point was another fork, — the left hand, running towards the mountain, led to the houses of Joseph Cutter, junior, John Cutter, second, and Daniel Cutter who afterwards, occupied the house built by Dr. Howe.

All these were sons of Joseph Cutter Esq. A Southerly branch turning off near Joseph Cutter, junior's, led to the houses of Joseph Mead, Mr. Brooks, David Cutter and Jacob Hammond.

The principal road, which turned to the right at the fork, led Northerly over the hill to a house owned by Joseph Thorndike. Esq., afterwards by John Conant, Esq., who has made himself widely and favorably known by his very liberal donations to divers public objects. It is now owned by the president of the day, — who speaks for himself.

The travel over the hill has since been diverted to the other branch, by a slight alteration, — in consequence of the modern discovery, (especially unknown to Turnpike proprietors in former days,) that in some cases it is no farther to go around a hill than it is to go over it, and that the larger load can be drawn on the level ground. Beyond, on the road to Dublin, were David Corey, Mr. Bullard and Mr. Johnson.

Of the other highways in the town, and the persons living upon them, my early recollections are of course less particular. I have a note of most of the inhabitants of the different sections, but for the location and even the names of many of them, I am indebted to Mr. Ethan Cutter, whose early opportunities for acquiring a full knowledge of the different localites were of the best, and whose memory of them is of the same character. Were there no reason but lack of time, I must leave this part of the subject to others who may be heard today, craving indulgence for subjoining a few notes respecting the Third New Hampshire Turnpike.

This Turnpike was incorporated in December, 1799, running from Bellows Falls, Vermont, to Ashby, Mass., fifty miles, and cost, it was said, fifty thousand dollars. It occupied portions of the old road in various places, — near the mountain, near the middle of the town, — and eastward of it. It struck off from the old road at John Cutter's tannery, and at Spofford's mills, and run by Col. Benjamin Prescott's tavern, in the East part of the town, and through "Tophet swamp" into New Ipswich.

The three men just named were marked men in their day. Mr. John Cutter carried on a large tannery, for that time, and made it a profitable business, which has since been enlarged. His children were among my old school-mates, and I am pleased to see some of them with us today. With the exception of Joseph Cutter, Esq., he has probably more representatives in town than any other of his contemporaries.

Deacon Eleazer Spofford, who purchased of Mr. Borland, his farm and mills, in 1778, was a tall gentleman of a grave demeanor, pleasant smile, and a kind heart, — I think universally beloved. He led the singing for very many years. If he had an enemy in the world, that enemy must have been an unreasonable man. He lost a young son in the burning of Rev. Mr. Ainsworth's house, in 1786. His mills were complete for that day. In the grist mill was a 'jack,' which if it was not the progenitor, was the prototype, of the modern elevator in hotels and stores. It was worked by water power, to carry the wheat, as soon as ground, to the bolter in the attic. A ride on it, with his son Luke, then miller, afterwards clergyman, was a treat to the boys who brought wheat to be ground.[*]

---

*Dr. Spofford says " He hàd for many years the best flouring mills in that part of New Hampshire.".
He removed to Bradford, Mass., now Groveland, in 1821, and died there in 1828.

A grandson of Deacon Spofford was Chief Justice of Louisiana at the time of the breaking out of the rebellion, and another is now Librarian of the Congressional Library.

There must have been some controversy respecting the location of the turnpike. In a poetical New Year's Address, sent from Parnassus to New Ipswich, soon after, it was said that the muse could relate, —

> "How Prescott and Merriam made a stand
> And bent the road to suit their land."

But she did not do it, and I can not.

Col. Prescott, as I remember him, was another of the tall men of Jaffrey, — of powerful frame, — and an influential man in the town. If any man could bend a turnpike, he might be expected to do it.

The principal taverns on the turnpike were those of Sweetser in Marlboro', — Milliken, Danforth and Prescott, in Jaffrey, — and Merriam and Batchelder in New Ipswich, celebrated honses in their day.

It was one of the principal thoroughfares from Central Vermont to Boston, and the transportation over it in the winter was, of course, quite large, as the route through Rindge was not then a great highway. This winter transportation was generally by two horse teams, attached to square lumber boxes, so called, loaded on the downward transit principally with pork, grain, beans, butter, cheese, and other country produce; and on their return trip with iron, molasses, rum, sugar, codfish, and other groceries. The dry goods of that day were principally of home manufacture.

Occasionally a severe storm, blocking the roads badly, would compel these teams to stop at the nearest of the taverns named, where the loggerhead was always in the fire in winter, and the landlord ready to make a "good stiff mug of flip."

Some of my auditory may not have heard the name before. It was concocted of home made beer, well sweetened, —a suitable proportion of West India rum, — and heated by the loggerhead to a proper temperature. When an egg was beaten in, it was called "bellows top," partly perhaps from its superior quality, and partly from the greater quantity of white froth that swelled up on the top of it.

With ten or fifteen teamsters gathered together by one of these snow blockades, and a fair allowance of flip, of course "the mirth and fun grew fast and furious;"—and when the storm was over, and the road began to be "broken out" the long line of teams, especially those ascending the hills to the West, was something to see.

The mail stage between Keene and Boston, for a long time, run over this road,—once a week,—twice,—daily, except Sundays,—then a despatch line, called the telegraph,* through in twelve hours,—superseded by the Railroad through Fitchburg; so that the crack of the stage driver's whip, and the blast of his horn, no longer echo among the hills.

The wayside inn, for the accommodation of the passing traveller, has fallen from its high estate, through the introduction of the railroads; and from the same cause, along with the introduction of other beverages, the institution of temperance societies, and the passage of prohibitory laws, the glory of Flip has departed, and its name is almost forgotten.

The turnpike was not a source of great profit, and was finally laid out as a common highway, the towns paying the proprietors a moderate sum in damages.

The beautiful and busy village of East Jaffrey, with its large cotton factory, and divers other manufactures, its hotel, stores, bank and dwellings, and with a railroad running through it, is comparatively of modern creation.

A short time since, I summed up my recollections of its people and business,—as I first knew it:—Dea. Spofford, and his mills,—Abner Spofford, and his blacksmith shop,—and Joseph Lincoln, and his clothier's shop.—William Hodge and his farm constituted a Northern suburb.

I must not omit to mention Amos Fortune. He was born in Africa,—brought to this country as a slave,—purchased his free-

---

*This line was established by Col. French, then of Keene, now of Peterboro'; and Col. Shepherd, then of Boston, now of Manchester.

dom,—purchased and then married his wife,—came to this place in 1781,—and lived subsequently about a mile Northeast of Spofford's mills, where he had a small tannery.

At that time any person who had come to dwell within a town, and been there received and entertained by the space of three months, not having been warned to depart by some person appointed by the selectmen, was reputed an inhabitant, and the proper charge of the town in case he came to stand in need of relief. This power of " warning out " was given to the towns that they might protect themselves against pauperism; and in some towns the selectmen were so careful of the interests of the town, that they warned all new comers to depart,—so zealous, that in one instance, as I have heard, the town having settled a minister, the selectmen forthwith warned him out.

Such general warnings were not practiced in this town, but Fortune was warned out in Sept. 1781, doubtless from an apprehension that he might become a pauper. Like all other persons similarly notified, he disregarded the warning, and he lived here the remainder of his life. Dying in 1801, without children, at the age of ninety-one, as stated on his gravestone, (which, as I recollect him, an active business man, seems to me doubtful at least,) he by his last will, after a provision for gravestones, another for the support of his wife during her life, and a small legacy to an adopted daughter, empowered his executor Deacon Spofford, if there was any remainder of his estate, to "give a handsome present to the Church of which he was a member, and the remaining part, if any there be, to give as a present for the support of the school in School-House No. 8." The Church received under this bequest in May, 1805, $100,—partly expended in the purchase of a communion service,—still in their possession ; and in September, 1809, the Judge of Probate ordered $233.95, the balance in the hands of the executor, to be paid over to the selectmen of Jaffrey, "agreeable to a special act of the legislature of the state of New Hampshire, passed on the 15th of June last." This act was passed because no person was mentioned in the will to receive and apply the fund. It is still

held by the selectmen in trust for the benefit of the District.—
We are aware that these sums represented much larger values
at that time, than like sums do at the present day. ·

We have come together, with hearts full of thanksgiving to
the Great Disposer of Events, that He has permitted us to as-
semble here, to commemorate the organization of civil institutions and government in our beloved municipal homestead.
But an occasion like this cannot be one of unmixed joy.

> " Time rolls his ceaseless course."

> " Still it creeps on,
> Each little moment at another's heels,
> Till hours, days, years and ages are made up,
> Of such small parts as these, and men look back
> Worn and bewildered, wondering how it is."

> " When in this vale of years I backward look,
> And miss such numbers, numbers too of such,
> Firmer in health and greener in their age,
> And stricter on their guard, and fitter far
> To play Life's subtle game, I scarce believe
> I still survive."

Death has removed, not only all the early inhabitants, and
many who were familiar with the history of a later date, because
principal actors therein, but many who, if less conspicuous, were
not less dear to us : and we pause a moment to dwell with a reverential remembrance, — with filial affection, — with devoted
love, — on the memory of those whose animated faces would have
greeted us at this time, had they been spared to this day.   Alas,
—for them, time is no more.

The sum of human joys and human sorrows, which have been
felt within the limits of this town during the past century, can
only be known to Omniscience.   The joys have passed, and are
passing, with little or no record of their existence.   And so of
many, perhaps most, of the sorrows.   But there is a parcel of
ground, of small extent, on the brow of the hill, and adjoining
the Common, which contains records reminding us of the sorrows of ourselves and others, which are of a more enduring
character.

There rest the remains of my beloved and venerated parents, my father dying at the age of seventy-eight, and my mother living until near ninety-seven. Other fathers and mothers, of like ages, are gathered there, shocks of corn fully ripe, and fit to be garnered; whom we must mourn, but with the consolation that they had done their duty in the community,—had fought the good fight,—had finished their course,—had kept the faith.

But these records tell other tales. There repose the husband and father, the wife and mother, who fell by the wayside, in the meridian of life;—who appeared to have before them years of happiness and usefulness to themselves and others,—upon whom young children were dependent, and to whom friends looked for counsel and for guidance.

Brothers and sisters, young men and maidens, who were just entering upon the threshold of existence, with a life of usefulness and honor and prosperity in anticipation, lie there side by side.

What agonies of grief, suppressed and irrepressible, have rent the hearts of survivors, as the mournful processions have passed within the gate, and consigned the remains of the beloved objects to their places of final rest.

Hallowed be the spot where the dust of the century is gathered together, and around which is clustered a century of the greatest of human sorrows.

Whatever of sadness may be in the retrospect, it is meet that we should celebrate the hundredth anniversary of an organization fraught with so much of usefulness to the persons who have lived within its limits.

We are here on a day that marks an era.

Let us rejoice that this town incorporation will be continued for the benefit and advantage of the generations who are advancing to its possession.

Let us rejoice that we may go onward into the new century. though it be to some of us but for a short period, and to none of us to its close; and that space is yet granted us to do something, not only for the comfort and welfare of those who are dear to us, but of the community around us.

And now, assembled here as the surviving representatives of the first century of our incorporation, and standing just within the threshold of its successor, let us dedicate this new municipal century, in which the town and its in-dwellers are to do service for another hundred years, to the prosecution and extension of every good and beneficent work of its predecessor.

I feel assured that you will join with me when I say :—We dedicate it to the promotion of Religion.

Not a religion which leans upon the State for its support, and depends upon faith without works; — but that religion which sustains the State by the inculcation of truths which lie at the foundation of organized and orderly society, and supports the government by its works. Not that religion which has its greatest regard for forms and ceremonies, and the washing of cups and platters; but that which sanctifies the heart and purifies the life.—Not that religion, if such there be, which enters into embittered controversies about dogmas, and disputes zealously about trifles; but that religion which being first pure, is "then peaceable, gentle, easy to be entreated, full of mercy and good fruits;" and which teaches the love of God with our whole heart, and the love of our neighbor as of ourselves.

We dedicate it to education and sound learning.

Not that learning which attempts from metaphysical nothings to make up a unit,—the votaries of which, multiplying themselves by themselves, think that they sum up the infinite, and something beyond;—but that learning which leads to the belief, in the language of the arithmetical aphorism of Parson Wigglesworth, of Malden, that

> "Naught joyn'd to naught can ne'er make aught.
> Nor cyphers make a sum.
> Nor finite to the infinite.
> By multiplying come."

Not to that training which leads self-sufficient people to attempt to magnify themselves, by multitudes of projects for making a new world different from, and thus better, than that which God made;—but to a system of education which has due regard to the nature of things, and to the constitution of mankind, and the ends which the Creator intended they should pursue; and which seeks by measures consistent with creation, as it exists, to perform the whole duty which the Creator requires, in the world as he has made it.

Not to that theory of education which proposing that all persons should be educated up to the utmost limit of which they are capable, becomes a practical and mischievous humbug;—but to that theory which shall provide an education of the highest character for all the members of the community, with reference to the needful discharge of the various employments and duties which must necessarily exist.

Not to that system of education which by "raising the standard," as it is called, subjects the young to such demands upon their intellect, in the time of their immaturity, as to impair if not destroy the physical powers, and thereby render intellectual acquisitions useless;—but to that system which recognizes the physical as well as the intellectual, and seeks to develop both according to their necessities,—and this not by subjecting first the one and then the other to an extraordinary strain, but by a moderation that shall be known in all things.

Not to that education which casts odium upon labor, and induces young men and women to endeavor to escape from its wholesome, invigorating influences, by a resort to cities for the purpose of begging for a situation, where ease shall lead to poverty; or which seeks, through political partisanship, for some petty clerkship under Government, leaving the successful incumbent without occupation, or the means of an honest livelihood, when the office falls into the hands of the next eager aspirant, who has pushed him from his official stool; but that education which dignifies labor, and seeks to improve its modes of action,—which qualifies the recipient to occupy his place in life, whatever it may be, and with cheerfulness and alacrity to do the duty which the State and the community demand of him.

May I add a constitutional provision.

Not to that learning which endangers the compromises of the Constitution by attempts to maintain that the United States were a Nation before they were States, and that the Constitution was formed by that Nation; — nor that other learning which would make shipwreck of Constitutional rights and safeguards, by theories which sophistically give to the War Powers of the President and Congress a predominance over Constitutional guaranties, — but that learning which accepting the undisputed facts of history, arrives at the conclusion that the Constitution was adopted by the several peoples of the different States, whereby the peoples of those States became a Nation for the purposes manifested by it, — and that the war powers, designed to preserve, cannot be rightfully exercised to destroy, the liberties of the people.

We dedicate it to Philanthropy and Charity.

Not to that philanthropy which consists in words and eschews works; not to that charity which, beginning at home, ends in the same spot; nor that charity which does hope things are not quite so bad as they are reported, but is fearful that they may be worse; — but to that philanthropy which does the deeds of the Good Samaritan, and which is open-hearted and open-handed within the limits of prudence; and to that charity which suffereth long and is kind, which envieth not, is not easily provoked, thinketh no evil, hopeth all things, and endureth all things.

We dedicate it to Ambition.

Not that ambition which seeks a seat in Congress by bribery, or any other seat by the petty arts of the partisan politician; — but that ambition described by Lord Mansfield, when he said, — "I wish popularity, but it is that popularity which follows, not that which is run after; it is that popularity which, sooner or later, never fails to do justice to the pursuit of noble ends by noble means."

We dedicate it to rational Amusement.

Not to the games or pursuits which blunt the conscience, deprave the habits, enervate the mind, and vitiate the taste; — but to the recreations which solace from care, stimulate the fancy, develop the muscle, sustain the nerves, and give, through social intercourse, a relaxation from toil, a kindly regard for our neighbors, and courtesy to our associates, whether within or without the township.

We dedicate it to the wise and just exercise of all the political and municipal Rights conferred upon the Town; and to the faithful discharge of all corresponding Duties.

Finally, as the sum of all, we dedicate it to Human Happiness, and the Glory of God.

And may His blessing rest upon it, and hallow it, from its commencement to its termination.

APPENDIX A.

NOTE TO PAGE 15. — A portion of Jaffrey was included in the original location of Peterborough.

The township of Peterborough was granted by Massachusetts, to inhabitants of that Colony, with power to the grantees to select the particular location. Under the erroneous supposition that the line between Massachusetts and New Hampshire was that claimed by the former, the grantees made their location beyond the jurisdiction of Massachusetts, and embraced within their "six miles square" a large portion of the valley between the base of the mountain on the east, (now known as Peterboro' mountain), and the Monadnock.

When it was ascertained that the location was within New Hampshire, and fell within the purchase of the Masonian Proprietors, Jos. Blanchard, as their agent, cut off a range and a half on the western side, in order to provide for a tier of townships east of the Monadnock, and the portion thus cut off was included in Monadnock Nos. 2 & 3, (Jaffrey and Dublin).

The Masonian Proprietors not only released the residue of the township to the grantees under Massachusetts, but gave them, to make up their quantity, a strip of land on the East, of equal extent to that taken off on the West. This however, being on the eastern mountain, was comparatively worthless. — The grantees of Peterboro', in grateful recognition of the kindness of the Masonian Proprietors in confirming so much of their invalid title, and in giving them an addition to make up their quantity, gave the Proprietors several lots in the township, — but they took care to locate them all in the new addition, on the east! — *Ex relatione Dr. Albert Smith.*

PPENDIX B.

NOTE TO PAGE 24. — Something more may be said upon this subject, and as I have no wish to recur to it again, I add here :

The compact made on board the Mayflower, which furnished the foundation of the first Town organization, — at Plymouth, was "occasioned, partly by the discontented and mutinous speeches of some of the strangers" on board the ship, and partly by the reason that "such an act by them done, (this their condition considered) might be as firm as any patent, and in some respects more sure." The matters which "occasioned" the compact had, therefore, no particular relation to the church polity.—It recited that they were loyal subjects of King James, that they had undertaken for the glory of God, and advancement of the Christian faith, and honor of their King and country, a voyage to plant a Colony,—and by it they combined themselves together, into a civil body politic, for the better promotion of those ends, and by virtue of it, "to enact, constitute and frame such just and equal laws, ordinances, acts, constitutions and offices from time to time, as shall be thought most meet and convenient for the general good of the Colony."

There is nothing, either in the reasons given for the act, or in the purposes of the expedition as recited, or in the agreement actually executed, which indicates that it was derived from the church organization,—or which in any way refers to the Congregational polity, or to any particular administration of church government,—and this, taken with the statements which are contained in it, tends to show that the town organization in Plymouth, which arose from it, was not even suggested by the clerical.

Quite consistently with this origin of the Town organization, there might have been a different church polity previously, and any church polity which the signers pleased, might have been adopted afterwards. The church polity of the same people, had, as a matter of course, a similar foundation, that of self-government,—but that fact did not of itself originate or give rise to the civil polity. It only accompanied it, each acting within its own sphere.

This organization of Plymouth became substantially a State, as well as a town. But the State was for the purpose of general government, and did not derive its ideal from the church; and when, by reason of the extension of the settlements, other towns were organized, it was for the purpose of ordering and managing their local affairs,—the support of religious teachers, along with the making and mending of highways,—the support of schools,—the preservation of the peace, through the instrumentality of the constable,—and the prevention of of trespass by cattle, through the institution of pounds.

The principle of self-government upon which the original settlement was founded, and upon which in reference to their local affairs, the Towns were afterwards organized, was not only a fundamental principle with the emigrants, but was a necessity under the circumstances attending the emigration. No one had authority to rule,—there were no means of government except by agreement, or force,—and they agreed upon a government for themselves, to be administered by themselves. It must have been the same if no church had then been organized among them. The same principle operated in regard to the church.— When the people broke from the authority of the bishops there was no authority in ecclesiastical matters, except their own, and thus Congregationalism came into existence.

It may be said, (and it seems to be the only *argument* which can be used in favor of the position), that the principles of the churches "led to this form of government,"—that the church organization was first, and that the Town coming after, adopted the same principle of self-government. To this "*Post hoc, sed non propter hoc,*"—*after*, but not *by reason* of the church organization, is a sufficient reply. There must be something more than this, to sustain the assertion that "it was a Congregational Church meeting, that first suggested the idea of a New England Town meeting."

Meetings of subscribers to the Compact made on board the Mayflower, grew out of the Compact itself.

APPENDIX C.

NOTE TO PAGE 38.—Attempts to manufacture cotton, by machinery, were made in this country as early as 1787, and in subsequent years in that century. The machinery was imperfect and the results, of course, unsatisfactory. The first mill, in New

Hampshire, was established in 1804, in New Ipswich. The first cotton mill in Peterboro' was incorporated 1808. It spun and sold yarn, but for years manufactured no cloth.—For these dates I am indebted to a small volume entitled, "Introduction and Early progress of the cotton manufacture in the United States," written by Samuel Batchelder, Esq., a native of Jaffrey, and published in 1863. Prior to the manufacture of cloth here, the cheaper cotton cloth, in the market, was a sleasy fabric, manufactured in India and England,—the latter heavily starched, to conceal its flimsy texture.

Enquiries in several directions enable me to add some information respecting the manufacture of Woollens.

It appears that a mill, a fulling mill I presume, was erected at Rowley, Mass., as early as 1643, but machinery for carding, spinning, and weaving was of a much later date. Carding machines were introduced into this country about 1794,—into New Ipswich in 1801, and probably soon after into this town. They had then been known in England twenty or thirty years. Some of the first carding machinery used in this country was shipped from England, as hardware, being exported contrary to the laws in force there. See Bulletin of Wool Manufacturers, April–June, 1873, page 193. Article by S. B.

T. Clapp, Agt., Pontoosuc Woollen Mill, Pittsfield, Mass., writes under date of October 9th, that Arthur Schofield started his first carding machine there in 1801;—that the first broadcloth made in this country was made by him, in that town, in 1804,—and that "in 1808 Schofield manufactured thirteen yards of black broadcloth, which was presented to President Madison, from which his inaugural suit was made. Fine merino sheep were introduced about this time into this town, and Schofield was able to select wool enough to make this single piece, and President Madison was the first President who was inaugurated in American broadcloth."

An extended, and very interesting, article on the subject, appears in the Boston Commercial Bulletin, of Nov. 15th, (as these sheets are passing through the press), which states that Arthur and John Schofield came to this country from England in 1793, and took up their residence in Charlestown, — that after looking around a few weeks they determined to make a start in the manufacture of wollen cloth by hand, — that John built the first machinery himself, and having completed " a hand loom, spinning jenny, &c., on the 28th of October he sold the first product of this loom, 2 1½ yards of broadcloth [?] for £16–16s., and 20 yards of mixed broadcloth for £12 ;"— that they removed to Newburyport in that year, for the purpose of starting a factory with improved machinery, and built a carding machine, which was first put together in a room in *Lord* Timothy Dexter's stable, and then operated by hand, for the purpose of showing its operation. " This was in the year 1794, and was the first carding machine for wool made in the United States ; and at this place were made the first spinning rolls carded by machinery."

A factory was started by them, and others, in Byfield, in 1795. A single carding machine and two double ones were placed in it. " A coarse kind of flannel called baize " was woven. What other cloth was manufactured is not stated.

They established a factory at Montville, in Conn., about 1798.

It appears further that in 1801, Arthur, having removed to Pittsfield, had a carding machine there, — advertised for wool to card, — and built carding machines for other persons.

It is then stated, " The first broadcloth made by Arthur Schofield after his arrival in Pittsfield was in 1804. The cloth was a gray mixed, and when finished, was shown to different merchants, and offered for sale but could find no purchasers in the village. A few weeks subsequently, Josiah Bissell, a leading merchant in town, made a voyage to New York, for the purpose of buying goods, and brought home two pieces of Schofield's cloths, which was purchased for the foreign article. Schofield was sent for to test the quality, and soon exhibited to the merchant his private marks on the same cloth which he had before rejected."

Then comes the statement respecting the manufacture of broadcloth in 1808, which President Madison wore when inaugurated.

Considering all these statements the reasonable conclusion appears to be, that the first *broadcloth* manufactured in this country was made in 1804, by Arthur Schofield, as stated by Mr. Clapp. It seems improbable that the cloth manufactured in Charlestown in 1794 could have been *broadcloth*.

At the period of which I speak, wool was carded partly by hand, but the carding machines generally turned out the rolls, which were spun upon the domestic great wheel, and woven in the loom, like the cotton, and then fulled and dressed by the clothier.

The great wheel and the loom have disappeared before their gigantic competitors ; and the linen wheel, which spun the flax,— humble little machine,— has gone along with its larger companions, although large linen manufactures have not succeeded in establishing themselves here to any great extent. — The preparation of the ground, the seed and the sowing, — the pulling, rotting, breaking, swingling and hatchelling of the flax, — with the spinning and weaving superadded, — involved too great an amount of labor for a successful competition with the foreign manufacturer, as soon as the profit from other branches enabled the farmer to purchase the foreign article, manufactured where labor is so much cheaper. — Besides, the manufacture of cotton cloth, by machinery, reduced the cost of that, so that it superseded the use of linen, in a very great degree.

RESONANT cheers were given as Boston "men of high degree" filed in at 11.30 A. M., and took seats upon the platform after a pertinent introduction by President Cutter. The party included Mayor Henry L. Pierce, Alderman L. R. Cutter, (chairman of the board who bore the visitors' expenses), Gibson, Brown and Sayward; John A. Haven, president, and Nathaniel J. Bradlee, ex-president of Cochituate Water Board; Alfred T. Turner, auditor of accounts; Joseph Davis, city surveyor; H. A. Blood, Superintendent of the Boston, Clinton & Fitchburg Railroad; President Howe of the Bedford & Taunton Railroad, and four companionable reporters representing the Boston *Post*, *News*, *Globe* and *Advertiser*.

The President then said: — The breezes that play around old Monadnock, so like the elixer of life to the weary wanderer, have called to us, among many others, a lady noted for her vocal powers. She has kindly consented to favor us with a song. I now introduce to this audience, the sweet songstress from the "Old Bay State,"

MRS. ANNA GRANGER DOW.

Mrs. Dow then sang "The Heavens are Telling," with telling effect.

The President then introduced the REV. RUFUS CASE, who read

A ·P O E M ,

BY MISS MARY BELLE FOX, OF JAFFREY, N. H.

A hundred times has Autumn seen
    His forest branches stripped and bare ;
A hundred times, when winds blew keen,
    White Winter's snows have filled the air ;
A hundred times Spring's magic wiles,
    Have clothed with green the hillsides brown ;
And now the last fair summer smiles
    That rounds the century of our Town.

Yon mountain calls to us to-day,
    And draws us with persuasive voice,
"This is your Town's memorial day,
    My children, keep it and rejoice :
While waving tree, and rock, and hill,
    With silent voices manifold,

Greet those who dwell among them still,
    And those who knew them well of old."

" Come, stand, as on my breezy height,
    And view the backward-sweeping past,
Then read your own deeds in the light
    The lives of others on them cast ;
And let old memories stir your hearts,
    Like breezes whispering through my pines,
Till the unbidden tear-drop starts,
    To read time's half-effaced lines."

And gladly we that call obey.
    And gladly do we gather here,
Turning our faces toward that way
    Whence shall the past's dim forms appear.
But who can lift with steady hand
    That misty curtain hanging low,
Shrouding the half-forgotten land,
    That far, dim land of long ago?

Not one among us here can see
    So far adown the winding way,
And say, " I do remember me
    What was on our Town's natal day ;
When people cried, ' God save the King,'
    Though freedom's pulses stirred their breast ;
Though swelled the seed about to spring
    Of our great nation of the West."

A stalwart band of men were they,
    The early settlers of our Town,
Loud rang their axes day by day,
    That hewed the forest monarchs down.
Men not afraid of honest toil,
    They sought the wilds a home to win,
And gladly from the virgin soil
    Gathered their harvest treasures in.

They built them houses large and plain,
    Where clustered their life's richest joys ;
Where round them rose a numerous train
    Of healthy, happy girls and boys.
That children's minds have need of food,
    That they may grow, full well they knew,
And built the district school-house rude,
    Wherein rich fruits of knowledge grew.

They felt the goodness of the Lord,
    Whose hand had led them all their days,
And gladly built with one accord,
    A house where they his name might praise.
Here still that ancient building stands,
    Scarce changed in outward form appears,
Unharmed by the destructive hands,
    Of near a century's changeful years.

'Twas when they raised that frame-work strong,
    One fair June morning, calm and still,

They heard,—or fancy led them wrong,—
  The far-off guns at Bunker Hill;
Whence rose that patriotic wave
  That o'er the land impetuous swept,
Waking in hearts of all the brave
  The love of freedom that had slept.

Quickly our fathers stirred them then;
  They left their homes, and took the gun,
And bore their part, as valiant men,
  In that long strife that freedom won.
Then with " clear shining after rain."
  The sun of peace dispersed their fears,
And in their quiet homes again,
  Passed on their uneventful years.

Where are they now? The bell that swings
  In yon old tower the tale doth tell,
Whene'er with solemn tone it rings
  Some parted soul a funeral knell;
Each to the grave has journeyed on,
  There each in lasting quiet sleeps,
The while his white memorial stone
  The door of his low dwelling keeps.

In yonder " city on the hill "
  The blooming sod above their breasts,
Where all is peaceful, calm, and still,
  Their pastor with his people rests.
Life held him here a hundred years,
  And kept him from his heavenly crown,
Till weary with its griefs and fears,
  He laid the heavy burden down.

O, friends, who seek in vain to-day,
  Some long-remembered, well-known face,
Perchance ye on yon marbles may
  An answer to your questions trace.
For sleep our fathers not alone,
  Full many of their children too,
Have crossed life's boundary, one by one,
  And paid the debt to nature due.

There rest our sons in hallowed graves,
  Who fell 'neath war's red, cruel hand;
Who gave their brave young lives to save,
  From traitor's foul designs our land.
O honored sires! O household dead,
  O soldiers true, sleep calm and sound!
Life bears us on with steady tread,
  On to the rest that ye have found.

Full well we know that this, our town,
  Has little worth in stranger's eyes,
We love it, for it is our own,
  And holds us by a thousand ties.
Here peace and plenty mark our lot,
  Now, e'en as in " the good old time,"

And Change and Progress question not
  To lay on us their hands sublime.

N'er entered in our father's dreams,
  Some changes that the years have wrought;
Our locomotives rush and scream,
  A fearsome thing they would have thought.
No prophecy the housewife's wheel
  Sung to them of the jarring looms,
That ply their giant frames of steel,
  In our tall factory's many rooms.

Our merry streams, that down the hills
  Go leaping on their sea-ward way,
Are caught and held by busy mills,
  Whom, willing subjects, they obey;
There great stones crush the yellow corn,
  There clanging saws harsh tumult make,
Where trees put off their forest form,
  And shapes for our convenience take.

Here nature's ever open book
  Displays its pictured pages too,
Showing to all who choose to look,
  Many a goodly pleasant view.
No lack of beauty, rugged hill
  And rock-strewn field have need to own,
When o'er them Summer's hand of skill,
  A drapery of green has thrown.

Sweet is the blooming orchard's breath,
  Rich glow their boughs through Autumn's care;
Pleasant their shadowy trees, beneath
  The dwellings, scattered here and there.
Sunny the pastures, sloping down
  To grassy meadows, cool and low;
Grand the old woods, whose columns brown
  The golden sunshine sets aglow.

Our winding river brightly gleams
  'Mid green, low banks its waters lave:
And one clear, flowing mountain stream,
  Holds gifts of healing in its wave.
Our ponds, like fretted silver shields,
  Dropped by some fabled gods of old,
When worsted on celestial fields,—
  The woods, with leafy arms, enfold.

There the sweet water-lily lies,
  And in the wave her beauty sees;
There many a timid, wild bird flies,
  And sings in the encircling trees.
Near them, the pink Azalea breathes
  Her sweetness on June's balmy air;
And there the glossy Laurel wreathes
  Her virgin blossoms, pale and fair.

But what, Monadnock, shall we say
  Of thee, thou dear to every heart

That knew thee in its childhood's day,
  Ere life from nature grew apart?'
Thy silent eloquence, is fraught
  With meanings deep, and grandly true,
Unconciously, our young hearts caught
  And held them, better than we kuew.

For always in our later years,
  However far our footsteps roam,
Our mountain clear to sight appears,
  When fancy paints our early home.
Grand mays't thou seem to stranger's eyes,
  And strangers tongues thy praises sing;
We hold thee in our memories,
  And love thee like a human thing.

God of our fathers, unto Thee
  With humble gratitude. to-day,
We bow the reverential knee;
  And at Thy throne our homage pay.
We pray Thee, bless our native Town,
  From henceforth, as Thou hast of old;
And shower upon her children down,
  Thy mercies, great and manifold.

Though, when the coming century's years
  Have passed, a swift and changeful train,
Not one of all who gather here,
  Shall on the shores of Time remain;
May we in Thine own blessed land,
  Where life and joy shall never cease,
Beneath Thy trees of healing stand,
  And walk upon Thy hills of peace.

HYMN OF GRATITUDE.

BY MISS ERMINA C. CAMPBELL.

Sung by the Choir.

We come, O God, a happy throng,
  Our grateful hearts to raise,
With glad accord, in Swelling song.
  In sweetest notes of praise.

From out thy boundless store, O God!
  An hundred years have shed ·
Their gifts on us who breathe to-day,
  And on the sleeping dead.

How countless are the fragrant
    thoughts
  Which cluster round those years!
What toiling hosts have shared their
    joys,
  Their thronging hopes and fears.

With hearts that thrill with solemn
    awe,
  We pause upon our way,
To view once more the shrouded Past,
  And greet the new-born day.

The pæan of an hundred years
  Is echoing in each heart;
Its grandly sweet and solemn strains
  Will nevermore depart.

We come, O God! to render thanks,
  Our grateful hearts to raise,
With fervent homage and with awe,
  In sweetest songs of praise.

President Cutter "took the floor" for a moment and said : —

Ladies and Gentlemen: — As our friends from Boston can re-main with us only a short time, we propose to defer dinner until half past one, therefore I now introduce to you C. A. Parks, Esq., of East Jaffrey, as Toastmaster of the day.

TOASTMASTER PARK'S REMARKS.

Mr. President, Ladies and Gentlemen; Fellow Citizens of Jaffrey: — I am grateful for the honor you have conferred upon me in your selection of a Master for your "Centennial feast." It is an office the duties of which will afford me much pleasure and impose upon me little labor, for I regard it as my special prov-ince not to attempt any speech myself today, but simply to re-introduce to you some of your old friends and acquaintances whose voices were familiar in the years past, and whose count-enances you welcome here, where you have gathered in one common brotherhood to celebrate the one hundredth natal day of your mother town.

I am glad that I am privileged, through a right of adoption by Jaffrey, to be present on this occasion and to participate in these exercises by proposing a few sentiments of an appropriate char-acter for your consideration ; and I hope from the responses to which we may listen, we shall be able to gather much of profit-able entertainment, and that in the words of those whom Jaffrey is happy to remember and honor on this day, there will come to us all many fruitful lessons respecting the reminiscences of the past and many golden hopes for the future.

We are honored today by Boston in the presence here of her Mayor and her Board of Aldermen, a body of gentlemen whose position distinguishes them as Boston's most worthy representa-tives. A sentiment has been selected for the Honorable Mayor, suggestive not only of the geographical proximity of New Hamp-shire to the city over which he presides, but also of that honest gratitude and pride over Boston's high rank and increasing great-ness as a metropolis, in which Jaffrey may be permitted to share through those of her sons she has given the great city to enroll among her honored names. It is this : " Jaffrey enjoys the honor of not being entirely outside that circle of which Boston is the centre and the 'Hub.' And she is justly proud of the distinction which New England's largest city has in the past given to many of her sons." I have the honor of presenting to you the HONORABLE HENRY L. PIERCE, *Mayor of Boston.*

MAYOR PIERCE'S RESPONSE.

LADIES AND GETLEMEN : — I did not come up here today to address you, or indeed with any desire to do so. In fact I shrink from making an address, but I came on the invitation of my friend Alderman Cutter, whom Boston knows and respects, to meet with you on this day so interesting to you and all of us. The close of a century in the history of the world, the close of present century is one of the most interesting and among the most eventful of any that have marked the progress of the race. When we look back and see what has been accomplished in the world, and even in this country, and see that during that time we have separated from the British crown and observe the improvements that have been made, and which affect the welfare of the world at large, we must look back upon it with the greatest satisfaction. But we must also look forward and hope that the century to come will be crowned with equal results. Boston is proud of being considered the metropolis of New England, and she desires to express her hearty thanks for the many good, sound men who have been sent to her from New Hampshire, and who have helped increase her prosperity. She hopes she is worthy of what New England has made her in the past, and she hopes to be worthy of the support of New England in the future, and now ladies and gentlemen, I will only say I thank you all and thank my friend the son of Jaffrey, the Alderman, for the great pleasure he has given me in inviting us to be present on this occasion.

SENTIMENT No 2 : — " We welcome those who having gone from us have aided in sustaining the charater of the noble sons of New Hampshire for integrity, enterprise and success in business, in every part of our land." Having read the above sentiment, the Toastmaster introduced the next speaker : —

I have the pleasure of presenting to you as a respondent to this sentiment a gentleman of whom nothing need be said by me. He his known to you all. His native town is Jaffrey, where he is always warmly welcomed. In Boston where he has resided for a number of years, he is noted as a gentleman eminently successful in business and one whom his adopted city has delighted to honor for his superior ability and sterling integrity. I refer to the Hon. Leonard R. Cutter, Chairman of the Board of Aldermen of Boston.

ALDERMAN CUTTER'S RESPONSE.

You do me great honor, Mr. President, in asking me to respond to the sentiment just read. I sincerely regret that I am not better qualified to do justice to the subject. I can truly say that whatever of success has attended the efforts of those sons of New Hampshire who have sought fame or fortune in other States and other countries has been largely due to the honorable distinction in which their birth-place is held. The old-fashioned standard of morality and integrity has been so nobly maintained by those who have remained at home, that the wanderers carry with them a certificate of good character in the name of the State from which they hail, and that goes a great way toward assuring them success even among the Philistines. While our State has not, for obvious reasons, increased so rapidly in wealth and population during the last fifty years as some other sections of the country, it certainly has not fallen behind any section in those things which tend to a higher state of civilization, good government and right living; and in the mean time it has been furnishing in larger proportions, I believe, than any other New England State, the intelligent enterprise which has, as it were, annihilated time and distance and enabled us to do our missionary work in the far West, and at the same time keep good hours at home. There is one advatage, Mr. President, which we who go away from home have over those who stay, and that is the pleasure of returning; and we also acquire a keener appreciation of the natural beauties of our native place. Although I spent my youth here in the shadow of Old Monadnock, I never knew or imagined the grandeur of the scenery I was daily looking upon until I had an opportunity of comparing it with other places. There is something enobling in the presence of this scenery beyond the power of any works of man. And, living in these Pacific Railroad times, it is a sort of satisfaction to reflect that the works of nature here are upon such a gigantic scale that the profaning hands of railroad contractors are almost powerless against them. But, Mr. President, the occasion on which we have met brings up other scenes and other events than those which are merely amusing or ridiculous. We have, this day, together, turned our eyes back upon the places that knew us in our infancy and youth. To us New Hampshire presents something other than her granite hills; yes, sir, and something more interesting even than the grassy vales or the pearly brooks, or the silvery water sheets, that are associated with the past time of our early days. Dearer to us still than the imagery of those bright scenes is the memory of the friends that we first loved; those who nurtured us in infancy, who guided us in youth, who opened to us the avennes of knowledge, who warned us of the miseries of vice, and presented to us the inducements of virtue, and who made us what we are. Perhaps they still live to greet our occasional returns to the paternal home; or, perhaps we have been called to commit them to the silent bosom of earth. Be that as it may, our relation to them is sacred, and while the power of thought shall endure, the memory of their kindness will abide. In conclusion, Mr. President, I give you as a sentiment (and I do not expect any one to respond to it unless the Old Man of the Mountain should happen to be present), "The Hills of New Hampshire. If Napoleon could incite his soldiers to greater deeds of valor by the thought that forty centuries looked down upon them from the pyramids, how much greater should be the inspiration and the achievement of the sons of New Hampshire from the thought that the centuries from the begining of time, looked down upon them from their native hills."

SENTIMENT No. 3. — " The day we celebrate."

Response by Rev. Moses T. Runnels, of Sanbornton, N. H.

Mr. President, Sons, Daughters and Citizens of Jaffrey: — I confess to a strong, inherent partiality for Centennial days, like this. The Centennial celebration of old Peterborough awakened my childish enthusiasm, at the age of nine years, and I have since labored hard, as a resident of those places, to secure similar centennials at Orford in 1865, and at Sanbornton in 1871. But this, Mr. Chairman, is the first Centennial Day I have ever really *celebrated " con amore."* For I do love old Jaffrey, having claimed a residence here for twenty-five years from infancy. I gazed upon that noble mountain, from under the old pine tree on the hill-top of my grandfather's farm, as one of my earliest remembered acts ; and, having found it the chief outward attraction of my home the last eight years, that I could *there* view this same Grand Monadnock from garden walk or study window, at the distance of 60 miles, it is not strange that the promptings of my heart would not suffer me to be absent from this place to-day ; — that neither the most pressing engagements at home, nor yet the appalling announcement that I might be called upon for a speech, could deter me from this family gathering of the sons and daughters of Jaffrey.

As we have listened, with so much interest, to the able historical address, it has been your privilege and mine, brothers and sisters, almost to exclaim with Virgil's hero, " *Quorum pars fui!*" —" of which I was a part," — our individual life, — our vivid remembrance, sweeping back, as it does in my own case, over two fifths of the century now passed. And I can tell you, sir, from my experience here today, as compared with that on other similar occasions, it makes a difference whether a man engages in a celebration like this, as a mere spectator, or as an actor in the scene ; — as a temporary resident, or as a son of the town whose festivities he enjoys. And while these rare entertainments for mind and *body* (as I was about to say, expecting to speak after dinner) have been spread before us, and I have felt that I might turn to this presiding officer — or to others of the committee of arrangements, — and say to each, '*you* and I, sir, were playmates together;' or might add to many others in this vast assembly, 'with *you*, your brothers, or your sons I sported in artless childhood;' 'with *you*, your sisters or your daughters, I attended school in the happy days of youth;' '*your* children I remember as among my favorite pupils in that old red school-house under the hill;' I can assure you, Mr. President and gentlemen, that I have found myself all the more ready to rise and at least repeat the sentiment you have so kindly given me, if I did not respond to it, "The Day *we* Celebrate."

And what do we mean by 'the day we celebrate'? The actual day of incorporation as it *was?* Or this glorious day as it *is?* Perhaps we ought to claim that we are "*celebrating*" both days; the day that was, and the day that is. What *that* day was, we can not know beyond what the distinguished orator of today has told us. It is like our birthdays in this regard; with the important difference that we were not any of us *there at that time to see!* Each one's imagination must help him to picture a scene in Jaffrey 100 years ago; — and as the beautiful banner we have seen borne before us today reminds us that Jaffrey was incorporated "*August 17, 1773*," I have thought that the few scattered settlers then in town might have come together about three days afterwards, on the day *exactly* corresponding with this, to hold a sort of *congratulatory meeting!* The news of the " act " of incorporation has just reached them! They have gathered in their rough suits of skins or home-spun from their scattered log cabins, perhaps to some central cabin near this spot. From how different scenes, and in what dissimilar apparel have *we* assembled at our congratulatory meeting! *They* came, on foot, or on horse back, at the rate of two miles an hour, through pathless forests or guided by scarred and jumping over fallen trees. *We* have come in our light pleasure wagons at the speed of six or eight miles an hour, or, upon the wings of steam at the rate of 500 hundred miles per day!

Those strong minded fathers, as they passed their hearty congratulations on the incorporation of their town, may also have spoken together of those ominous mutterings of an approaching revolution of which they were hearing from week to week, from the then distant city of Boston, — perhaps of the late tea-party

there. We, their descendants, if we think of any centennial besides our own, are perhaps letting our thoughts go forward to
that grandest of all the days in our nation's history, if God permit, the approaching hundredth anniversary of the Declaration
of her Independence. And of what surprising *changes* are we
thus reminded, as occurring *between* these "days we celebrate,"
in the nation, in the town and in social life!

But on many other accounts is *this* "day we celebrate" interesting and valuable to us all.

It affords an opportunity for the *renewal* of *old associations*, —
the fondest and dearest of our earthly lives, in those scenes and
times of our earliest recollection when we could speak of joys
unmingled with sorrow. Who of us does not hasten to recall
the loves and friendships of those early days, so pure — so pro-
ductive of a happy state — so free from the alloy of selfishness!

For how many *reunions* of *later friends,* long separated from
each other, does this day also afford the glad occasion. It would
seem as if the orbits of our lives, having run for many years at
a distance from and out of sight of each other, were now brought
into a mutual and delightful juxta-position; or, like vessels at
sea, bound on the same voyage, after having, in separation, out-
ridden many of the storms of life, we are today permitted to
course for a few hours within "speaking" distance of each other, — to compare notes on all the way in which a kind Providence has led us, each in our several spheres of duty, — to rejoice in each other's prosperity, — to sympathize with each other's griefs.

And this reminds us, again, of the *dear ones* "*not lost,*" as we
fondly hope, "but gone before," with whom we formerly "took
sweet counsel together, and walked," it may be, " to the house
of God in company." Does it not seem, my friends, as though
their spirits, if aught on earth can afford them happiness, might
even now be the unseen witnesses of this joyful re-union? At
least, are not their countenances, their loved or venerated forms,
their winning voices all fresh in our recollections today? Is not
our communion with them almost as palpable and as marked as
that with one another?

Once more "the day we celebrate" bespeaks our *great in-debtedness* to the ancestral fathers and guardians of the town in all previous years.

What this age is especially deficient in, is a respect for the past. But the celebration of this day is a practical application of the noble sentiment of Burke, — "Those who do not treasure up the memory of their ancestors, do not deserve to be remembered by posterity;" — though by no means exposing us to the quaint sarcasm of Sir Thomas Overbury, that "those who rest *their claim to consideration* on the merit of their ancestry instead of their own individual worth, are like a hill of potatoes, — the best portion is under ground."

And how, in this connection, did time permit, would I love to pay my humble tribute to the fathers of Jaffrey, whose very images are now so vividly before me, as having been upon the stage a third or half a century ago! How many honored names do I recall! The Ainsworths, the Parkers, the Spauldings, the Gilmores and the Howes; the Cutters, the Baileys, the Law-rences and the Emerys; or in the other part of the town where I lived, the Prescotts, the Spoffords, and the Joslins; the Pierces, the Bacons, the Mowers, and many others all over town who might be mentioned; with others still who hardly yet have passed from our view; and especially that prince among New Hampshire farmers,* — that prince among the benevolent benefactors of the town and the State at large, to whom *you* and *I*, Mr. Chairman, feel ourselves personally indebted for those habits of industry and that spirit of energy and enterprise which he early instilled within us, tempered ever with the most excellent counsels and confirmed by a most laudable example.

In view of *all* these noble men and women too, who have given character to the Jaffrey of the past, moulding her institutions, establishing her educational and religious privileges and adorning her homes, we can only exclaim, what a rich legacy is here! What cumulative influences and forces for good have come down to us from the record of the last century! How should this

---

*The Hon. John Conant, who, from feeble health, was unable to be present.

stimulate our gratitude for what the fathers and the mothers *were* and for what they *accomplished* in our behalf! And how zealous should we be to transmit what we have received, unimpaired, to those who shall come after us.

For, while to the aged, and those who review the past, the "day we celebrate" is so full of rich satisfaction, with how much of value is it also freighted to the *young* — even to these little children who have formed, in many respects, the most attractive part of our procession today! How much useful information may they gain from the day itself, its teachings and its suggestions! How much, otherwise unknown, may they learn, even respecting the fathers themselves. What insight will be afforded them into the habits of life and social ways of periods long past! And when they reflect upon the changes since effected, — the new discoveries and inventions, — the improvements in agricultural and mechanic arts and implements, — the increase of books and other appliances for obtaining and diffusing knowledge, — the improved facilities for travel and intercommunication, — the bringing together of the nations, and the progress and elevation of mankind, — all of which have been literally crowded into the space of the hundred years now closing; let them be encouraged to graft upon the moral and religious principles the sterling virtues, the heroic qualities of mind and heart which belonged to the fathers in the century past, — to *graft upon* these, I say, all that is inspiring, hopeful, and healthfully progressive in the new century of our local history now commencing.

Which leads me to add very briefly in conclusion; "the day we celebrate" is especially valuable to the *town historian*. I rejoice that old Jaffrey has one from whom we are to hear on this occasion. This day may well afford to him a fresh *nucleus*, — a new starting point, as it were; and the success of our historical orator today may give him new aid, impulse and encouragement to press forward in his noble work. Many are the difficulties which beset the path of the town historian. Great the apathy which broods over many minds; surprising the indifference which many manifest as to all, or aught that pertains to the past history of those localities — of those families, even, in which they themselves should naturally take the deepest interest. The dark clouds of mystery and uncertainty which are found hanging over the facts and records of the past are also quite disheartening at times : but these will usually be found lifting and unveiling themselves before the patient persevering historian, as he plods along, and often from the most unexpected sources and in ways before unthought of. The satisfaction and reward (not pecuniary) of the local historian's work are therefore very great. Its importance cannot be over estimated. It must be done quickly or it will never be accomplished ; and when *once* done and well done, it is done for ever ! Let facts, therefore, respecting the men and the things which ever belonged to this good old town be industriously collected and properly arranged. Let the genealogies of the old families be traced out, even into other towns and other parts of the country, so far as possible, for thus, much may be learned throwing light upon the history of the town itself. It will thus be known what an aggregate amount of influence the town has really exerted in building up other communities and moulding society in other localities. The gratification of all concerned will be great and ever increasing as years and generations in the future roll away ; posterity will approve the sayings and the doings of the faithful annalist. The stores of actual knowledge shall be increased ; different parts of our country shall be more effectually cemented together ; mankind shall be elevated, and the great God who has " been our dwelling place in all generations " shall Himself be glorified.

SENTIMENT No. 4. — " Jaffrey : Her Scenes and her Scenery." Response by Rev. J. M. H. Smith, of East Jaffrey.

An hour having been spent in social intercourse, and distributing among the many from the inexhaustible store of provisions until all were satisfied, the Tent Programme was resumed by the band's playing the " Ella Polka," after which Prof. George W. Foster sang a taking ballad —

" Dinna forget yer mither. Sandie,"

with brilliant success, when Tostmaster Parks proceeded to say ;

Ladies and Gentlemen : — After having partaken of the *material benefits* so bountifully provided for the inner man on this occasion, it is proposed that we resume again that other *feast* began before dinner, to wit: " The feast of reason and the flow of soul."

SENTIMENT NO. 5. — " The Orator of the day. — We have hitherto been proud of his name and reputation as one of the great lights of the legal profession; he has today placed us under infinite obligation for his interesting and eloquent address." Hon. Joel Parker rose and expressing his gratitude, for the honor bestowed upon him, said that another speech would not be expected from him today.   He asked leave to place in the hands of the Toastmaster the following Sentiment:—"The inhabitants of Jaffrey — Steadfast in their principles — Untiring in their Industry."

SENTIMENT No. 6. — " Our Common Schools."
Response by Rev. D. N. Goodrich, Sup't School Committee, Jaffrey, who said that while he need not remind a New England audience how highly THE FATHERS valued common school education, how they built the school-house close by the meeting-house to show, that in their opinion, religion and education should go hand in hand, he would mention some facts which indicate that the people of this generation value these interests just as highly as their fathers did, and are disposed to guard them with a jealous care.   Among other things, the speaker referred to the large number of schools in the town; the amount of money expended for their support, the average expense for each scholar being $5,25 and in some districts $16,45 ; the whole number of scholars being 360.   He mentioned also the fact that the schools were so frequently visited by the people in the various districts ; that so much pains is taken to procure good teachers ; that the teachers employed have generally been so well qualified, and that so many of them have received a large part of their instruction in our schools.   In conclusion the speaker thought the facts of the case and the views of the people might be expressed by offering the sentiments in the following form:
—" Our Common School System a priceless legacy received from

the fathers, perfected by the wisdom and experience of successive generations, and supported by the intelligent patriotism of our people; our teachers thoroughly competent, efficient, and devoted to their noble work; our school officers, assiduously guarding the precious interests committed to their charge; our scholars, the good material out of which intelligent, useful, and honorable members of society are to be made."

SENTIMENT No. 7. — " East Jaffrey Cornet Band : They may write 'Excelsior' on their escutcheons." Music : " Lepitit Polka."

SENTIMENT. No. 8. — " The Mothers and the Daughters; the Joy and Sunshine of our Homes and the Pride of the Century."
Response by A. S. Scott, Esq., of Peterboro', N. H.

Mr. President, Ladies and Gentlemen ; — When I accidentally read the announcement in our village newspaper by your Jaffrey correspondent, that I had been invited to respond on this occasion to a sentiment to the Ladies of Jaffrey, and had accepted the invitation, it was to me a matter of surprise, because it seemed to me more fitting that to one of the sons of these Jaffrey mothers, or one of the husbands or suitors of these fair Jaffrey daughters should have been assigned the privilege to speak to a sentiment so suggestive of all the sweet and dear remembrances that cluster around your old family homes among your hills.

Then, I should be excused from speaking here today, because of the acknowledged ability of these ladies, if this assembly could be resolved into a tea-party and they should once get their tongues loose, to speak for themselves.

But mothers and daughters of Jaffrey, discarding all empty compliments and flattery, so repugnant to your good sense, you will permit me to say that in these old family homes among these hills, presided over with such matronly dignity by the mothers, and made sunny and happy by the genial presence and affectionate smiles of the daughters, has been nurtured all that is good and memorable and great in the history of the century that has passed.

For these New England homes watched over by pious and devoted mothers are conceded to be the best manufactories of men. —But there is now very serious danger that this work of growing and training men must cease for lack of material. No one can have failed to observe the difference in the size of the families of the early mothers and the families of the present day. The former numbered from six to sixteen, and the latter from one to four.

In your school districts which were formerly densely populated with scores of ruddy boys and girls, you now are indebted to the Irish emigrants for children enough to make a school.

One of your early settlers, who, on his bridal tour, about a century ago, brought his wife to a log cabin in the wilderness in an ox cart, with her spinning wheel and other marriage outfit, raised in this cabin eleven children.

And these large families were beehives of industry and no drones were allowed in the hive. Father, mother, sons and daughters worked and sometimes more than ten hours each day.

There is not an honored descendant of these families here today who does not in all sincerity acknowledge himself more indebted for such measure of honor and success as has attended him on life's battle field, to the lessons and habits of industry and frugality, inculcated in the old home than to all other causes and influences combined.

John Conant, when, with matchless industry, perseverance and economy, he was laying the foundations of that wealth which has enabled him to endow your High School, a Seminary and an Agricultural College so munificently, gaining for himself an honored and illustrious name among the benefactors of his race, was largely indebted to the industry and frugality of his wife.

There is not a good thing that marks your progress during the century,—a school, a church, a library, or a reform,—that has not been largely fostered and helped onward by the labors and sacrifices of the mothers and daughters. Now, the *school-masters* having mostly gone abroad, almost the entire education of your children is committed to the daughters and no one doubts that they will be faithful to their responsibility.

The mothers and daughters have not at any time in the century been wanting in the exhibition of an exalted patriotism.

In the Revolutionary war they bravely sent their husbands to the front and remained at home faithful and devoted to their families, adding often to the labors of the household the labors of the field.

In the war of the Rebellion the mother heroicly severed the tie that bound her to her son and sent him forth to the service of his country with her prayers and benediction, and side by side with the recruiting station, organized the Soldiers' Aid Societies, the springs of the Sanitary Commission, the Good Samaritan of the war.

There is not a son of Jaffrey who has come up here from his home in another State to revisit the scenes of his childhood and live over in imagination his boyhood days, who does not bring in his heart some tribute of gratitude and respect for the mother who bore him, — who cradled him in her arms, — taught his infant lips to lisp his morning and evening prayer, and, as he grew into boyhood, patched his trowsers, washed his face, combed his hair and sent him to school on a week day, and bade him " mind the master, learn his lesson and bring home the medal;" and on Sunday, took him with her to church and made him read the Bible and say the catechism; and later, as he ripened into young manhood and manifested a love for learning, with gentle persuasion, influence the *pater-familias* to sell his cow, or yoke of oxen, to raise money to send him to college, — then with assiduous toil carded with her own hands the rolls, spun and dyed the thread, and on the old hand-loom, located up in the old attic to be out of the way of interruption, wove the fabric and then fashioned and sewed the suit in which her son entered the Academy or College.

And this is no fancy picture for the man still lives and will address you here today who entered Dartmouth College in a suit of home-spun manufactured entirely by his mother.

Many of these mothers still live to grace and honor this assembly with their presence, but many have passed away and been borne to their resting places in your village cemetery, and to many a son those beautiful lines of Cowper, addressed to his mother's picture, have come home with peculiar power.

> "My mother, when I learned that thou wast dead,
> Say, wast thou conscious of the tears I shed?
> Hovered thy spirit over thy sorrowing son,
> Wretch even then, life's journey just begun!
> I heard the bell tolled on thy burial day;
> I saw the hearse that bore thee slow away,
> And, turning to my nursery window, drew
> A long, long sigh, and wept a last adieu."

Many a son of Jaffrey has wept a last adieu at the grave of his mother, but her love and affection will hallow his latest as his earliest memory.

But I am admonished to close by the consciousness that the time of this occasion belongs to your own sons and not to me.

I give you as a sentiment in closing : — " The Mothers of Jaffrey ; Models of Industry, Piety and Frugality ;— May their Daughters emulate their Mothers' Virtues.

SENTIMENT No. 9. — "The Clergy of Jaffrey." Response by Rev. E. S. Foster, of Winchester, N. H.

Coming upon the platform at the call of the Chairman, Mr. Foster said : — " Every child, youth, man and woman, every settlement, society, village, partnership and business, every family, tribe, nation, country and government has a history. In the life-time of every individual, settlement, country and kingdom, there are various epochs of greater or less importance. Jaffrey, as a town, has had various epochs, among which are the pioneer, agricultural, ministerial, religious, educational, business and mechanical.

Today, in her history, this Celebration marks the one hundredth epoch. In the work assigned, I am called to speak for the ministerial department in the life of Jaffrey's hundred years.

"The Clergy of Jaffrey," is my subject. Here allow me to say, I would that that the work assigned me in this important and ever to be remembered occasion, had been given to other and abler hands, that the lessons of our life may sink deeper into the character of Jaffrey's coming children for devotion and consecration, than it is possible for me to impress and inspire.

But the noble soldier puts on his armor and takes the place assigned him; thus I remark, — First, from a competent person I have an extract from the records of Jaffrey, which is as follows, viz: — "28 Sept., 1773, Voted £6 Lawful money, to support preaching. 26 April, 1874, Voted £6 Lawful money, to support the Gospel. 13 April, 1775, Voted £6 Lawful money, to support the Gospel. 27 March, 1777, Voted £50 Lawful money, to support the Gospel. 26 March, 1778, Voted £100 Lawful money, to support the Gospel. 10 June, 1778, the Committee agreed with Mr. Isaac Allen to supply us. 3 Sept., 1778, the Committee omit giving Mr. Allen a call for the present. Sept. 3, 1778, Voted £50 for preaching. 11 Nov., 1778, Voted to hear Mr. Reed until special meeting. 25 March, 1779, Voted £200, to support the Gospel. 1 Nov., 1779, Voted to hear Mr. Stevens for all supply this fall. 1 Nov., 1779, Voted to have Mr. Colby come by 1st March next. 7 June, 1780, Voted to hear Mr. Jewett more on probation, in order to give him a call. 29 March, 1781, Voted not to hire Mr. Walker this year. 16 August, 1781, Voted to hire Mr. Goodale two more Sabbaths. 27 December, 1781, Voted to hear Mr. Ainsworth. 8 July, 1782, Voted to give him a call."

Foremost, longest, and fullest upon the ministerial record of Jaffrey, stands the labors of the long to be remembered Pastor— Rev. Laban Ainsworth. This ministerial pioneer was born at Woodstock, Conn., July 19, 1757. At about 7 years of age, an accident resulted in his losing his right arm and hand. He was educated and fitted for college under Nathaniel Tisdale, of Lebanon, Conn., — "a man of considerable pedagogical capability, and of much petulant eracibility." These last facts modified by the last word, are from Mr. Ainsworth's own language, in reply to some questions presented by a friend. Mr. Tisdale fitted him for Harvard College, but his father said, "to avoid the British, go to Dartmouth in the woods." He entered Dartmouth in 1775, and graduated in 1778. He studied Theology with Rev. Stephen West, D. D., of Stockbridge, Mass., and soon after, preached about two years in Spencertown on the Hudson River, then served from four to six months as Chaplain in Maj. McKinistry's Corps.

We find from the record that the Church in Jaffrey was organized May 18th, 1780, and that a committee from the town met Mr. Ainsworth on Commencement Day at Dartmouth, in 1781, and engaged him to preach; and he began the same summer. He was ordained the first minister in the town of Jaffrey, N. H., December 10th, 1782.

On December 4th, 1787, he married the daughter of Jonas Minot, of Concord, Mass., with whom he lived happily and successfully over fifty years, and labored as the minister of the First Congregational Church and Parish of Jaffrey, for over half a century.

On the 11th of January, 1832, he received Rev. Giles Lyman as his Colleague; with whom he lived pleasantly for a number of years. He died March 16th, 1858, after a life of an hundred years, and a ministry of about seventy-five years in all. The portraits which hang today in the parlor of his old home, are excellent representations of him and his wife when they were about seventy-five years of age.

His dress was thoroughly clerical black; single breasted coat and waist coat, black small clothes, black worsted stockings, shoes, knee-buckles, and shoe-buckles. In his advanced years, his long white hair and his courtly manners, made him a perfect representative of his class. As a preacher he was very simple in manner and matter; his voice was remarkably strong, clear and sonorus; his enunciation distinct, and his language pure Saxon English. In his religious views he was dogmatic and radical, and much of a doctrinal preacher, holding to the Calvinistic Theology, as taught by Dr. Edwards.

His sermons were seldom if ever written out in full; they were on paper, mere briefs, and very few of these remain. The only remaining one was here presented to the sight of the assembly. Its subject was an argument against final restoration. His sermons were very short; seldom exceeding 25 minutes. His pulpit services consisted of a hymn, a short prayer, reading of Scripture, hymn, the long prayer, the sermon and then the benediction.

His preaching and ministerial labors produced the usual amount of conviction and conversion. He must have attended about three thousand funerals; the services of which consisted generally of an address to the mourners, with an opening and closing prayer.

A wedding service he opened with prayer, then he gave the legal point, and lastly the address to the man and wife. As a politician, he was a Federalist, like Washington and Jefferson; in a later day he acted with the Whig party. On Fast days he usually gave his people something of a political discourse.

As a friend of education, he usually appeared in most of the District Schools during their closing days; but did not often fraternise much with the children and youth of the town.

As a man and minister, he commanded the respect and esteem of all classes. As one of the "*Mystic Tie*," he received this *lamb-skin*, or (here the original lamb-skin received at his initiation as a Mason was exhibited,) white leathern apron, which is an emblem of innocence, and a badge, more honorable than the star and garter, or any other order that can be conferred on the candidate at any time by king, prince, potentate, or any other person except a brother Mason. By this lamb-skin he was continually reminded of that purity of life and conduct which is essentially necessary to his gaining admission to the Supreme Temple above. Thus, being born when George 2d was his King, and in the time of Louis 15th, of France, Frederick the Great, of Prussia, and Clement 16th, of Rome, his life covered volumes of history.

Severel anecdotes were here related of the worthy divine, which extensively stirred the risibilities of the great assembly.

The next ministerial record, and the first of Jaffrey's born sons to the ministry, is that of Rev. Robertson Smiley, born at Jaffrey, graduated at Dartmouth, 1798. He was the settled minister of the First Congregational Church of Springfield, Vt., from a very early date, and died at that place in 1856. after a long, laborious and noble ministry.

Rev. Levi Spaulding was born at Jaffrey, August 22, 1791. graduated at Dartmouth College, 1815; studied Divinity at Andover, Mass., and went as a Congregational missionary to Ceylon in 1819. Here with one exception of a visit of three years to the U. S. he spent his life and labors in the Master's vineyard. He did much valuable work in a series of school-books, the compiling of a Dictionary, and the translation of the Bible into the native tongue of Ceylon. He died June 18, 1873, after a long life of neble christian warfare.

Rev. Luke Ainsworth Spofford, born at Jaffrey, Nov. 5, 1786, was fitted for College under Rev. Laban Ainsworth, his pastor, and Rev. Dr. Payson, of Rindge, N. H. He graduated at Middlebury College, Vt., in 1816. He studied divinity at Andover, Mass.; was first settled at Gilmantown, N. H., then at Brentwood, Lancaster and Atkinson, then filled the office of Missionary for some time, and afterwerd labored for years in the missionary field of the Western States, and died at Rockport, Ind., Sept. 27, 1855. Earnestly and devotedly he spent his life for man's salvation, and left an excellent record as a faithful minister of Christ.

Rev. Abel Spaulding was born at Jaffrey, Aug. 22d, 1791; graduated at Dartmouth, 1815; studied divinty at Andover, Mass.; was settled at Cornich, N. H., where he died a few years since, much beloved by his denomination — the Congregational, and esteemed for his good ministerial record.

Rev. James Howe was born at Jaffrey; graduated at Dartmouth College in 1817; studied Divinity at Andover, Mass., and was settled at Pepperill, Mass., where he spent his life as a faithful, devoted and esteemed minister of the Congregationalists, and died in 1840, aged forty-three.

Rev. Henry Shedd, born at Jaffrey; graduated at Dartmouth College in 1826; studied Theology at Andover, Mass., and has spent nearly his entire life as a home missionary in the Western States as a Congregationalist.

Rev. Adonijah Cutter, born at Jaffrey; studied Divinity at Bangor Seminary, Me., and settled in the Ministry of the Congregrtionalists at Strafford, Vl., in June, 1840: here he spent a ministry of ten years. Then for a time a minister at Hanover, N. H., being dismissed in 1857. He was soon after settled at Nelson, N, H., where he died in a short time, leaving a life of devotion and faithfulness.

Rev. —— Jaquith, born at Jaffrey; became a self-taught minister of the Baptist denomination in Maine, doing a good work, and is today on the field of missionary labor.

Rev. Wm. Dutton, born at Jaffrey, in 1815; fitted for College at Melville Academy, entered Brown's University at Providence, R. I., in 1839, and graduated in 1842, with much honor. He taught school several years at Kalamazo, Mich., and died in 1846, aged 30 years. For this noble man and promising minister for the Baptist denomination, too much cannot be said. Intensely industrious and studious, an honest and lively thinker, a devoted christian, he went down to an early grave, honored and beloved by all who knew him. Many on earth held his memory above price, and in glory did he pass to the spirit-land to receive the unfading Crown from the hand of the blessed Master.

Rev. Andrew O. Warren, born at Jaffrey; prepared for the study of Divinity at Melville Academy, entered on his theology course with J. V. Wilson in 1838, and completed it with Rev. Charles Woodhouse of Westmoreland, N. H., in 1840, and the same year entered the ministry of the Universalists. He has been located at McDonough, Upper Lisle, and Smithville, N. Y., then at Montrose, Pa., where, and in the region, he has been actively engaged in the ministry since 1849.

In 1860 he began the study of Law; was admitted to the Bar of Susquehanna County Court in 1862, and to the Supreme Court in 1865. And yet he has been continually in the Master's vineyard saving souls, and on week-days, in the world, stoutly contending for the salvation of men's wills from the ruins of avarice and self.

Rev. E. S. Foster, born at Jaffrey, Sept. 1821; was a student at Melville Academy, Lawrence Academy of Groton, Mass., and closed his academic education at Keene, N. H., in 1843. From this time till 1849, he labored in the mercantile business. And in September of this year, he entered the study of Divinity with Rev. O. A. Skinner, D. D., of New York completing the course in about four years. After much sickness he was ordained in June, 1855, at South Hartford, Washington County, N. Y., where he first settled. He has labored in Abington, Mass., Cuttingsville and Chester, Vt., at Claremont, N. H., at Middletown, Conn., and is now an active minister of the Universalist denomination at Winchester, N. H.

Thus much in brief of the history of Jaffrey's sons who have filled no ignoble place in the Christian Ministry as each has understood Christ and his scheme of salvation. I feel sure that they will compare favorably in body, talent and labor, with the same number of ministers selected from any town of equal population in New England.

Here allow me a few words for our calling, and I am done. I believe it can be shown that the Ministry of Christianty in the various Denominations, has done more to make Jaffrey in the life and character of her citizens, than all other influences combined.

Think for a moment! Here is the intellect, that a few years ago, in feebleness, and helplessness nestled in its parent's arms and could not utter the word *Mother ;* — but today, can survey broad acres, build and furnish the gorgeous home, rear and finish the lofty temple, plan and perfect cities, make and defend empires, girdle the earth in a few moments with its thought, and leave character behind which shall be a missionary of blessed life. We, today are what our parents and the christian ministry have made us.

Here fathers and mothers, brothers and sisters are our children, which all the wealth and empires of earth cannot purchase, and for whom you will give the last dollar, yea, and your life also, to defend from the grave. And they are in your hands, and the christian ministry to mould and educate, to tune and tone for nobleness and virtue in the world, and to prepare for the ineffible scenes of the incorruptable life.

Who among you can estimate the intellect of your child,— its probabilities and its possibilities in the coming days of earth?— Remember! all history teaches us that depression, misfortune and slavery cannot break it; ambition, empire and enormous riches and rule cannot conquer it; and the longest life and the best culture cannot fill the compass of its desire, or satisfy its capabilities.

This restless spirit, this irrepressible mind of your child is to-day for your shaping as clay in the potter's hand.

What stamp are you putting upon it! Is it that of mortgage bonds and government scrip, that will petrify the heart and curse with avarice and the long train of woes, the coming generations? Or is it the stamp of an honest and christian life of industry, that will charm the coming individuals in the grandest of all characters — the life that is Christ to live? Oh! what a gift is your child! What a gem of priceless value is its intellect, given to you as the artist who is to set it! And are you setting it? Are you setting it in the gilt of fashion and popularity, in game and Sabbath-breaking, vainly supposing that the canker of remorse will not consume it?

Are you setting it in the rough of profanity and avarice, idly assuming that the fires of retribution will not destroy it? Or are you setting it in virtue, cultivation and spiritual refinement, and under ministerial toning, feeling assured that God renders to every man according to his deeds?

Forget not I pray you, that a single man made the French nation, nominally all infidel. And another made them all warriors. A Carthagenian General put his little boy of ten years, upon the altar of his country and made him swear to be Rome's eternal enemy. And he was such until he sunk into the grave.

Now if such a mighty power lies dormant in your child, mould it to make the coming Jaffrey, or some other town to war for ever against ignoble character; and on the alter of humanity make that child to affirm understandingly that it will be the eternal enemy of all sin, depravity and crime. .

Remember the fact, — here is a common school teacher, the most of whose students, as they went from his hands to the business world, have been unfortunate in health and worldy matters. Here is another, most of the students of whom were sent into practical life, have been successful and happy, enjoyed much health, and occupied high positions.

How important then, to have the right education; what a need to have the best instruction toned into your children by a live, consecrated teacher, inspired by an energetic ministry!

Make the culture, whether from the school-room or the pulpit, so perfect, so entertaining and instructive that all the families around it shall be drawn to it as all the vegetable world is drawn up into life, beauty and worth by the sun! Into this cause should we collect all the stores of human learning, and reduce them to one rational, charming and useful body of science — of active business, and of honest, ambitious character, that shall be as light to those in darkness, as water to the thirsty, as bread to the hungry, and as life to the dead.

And the whole should be put under an affectionate, social, and instructive *ministry* that can fondle the darling child, stimulate and tone heaven-ward the fiery youth, and inspire the young man to cut his name on humanity in the noblest deeds of an honest calling. Then make its devotion in righteousness and labor so intense and permeating, that it will *assimilate* or *annihilate* the world of evil.

A celebrated painter of Italy was once asked by a friend, — "Why he spent so much time and labor in the study of the arts nd sciences; why he visited all Europe — the halls and galleries of all nations, and studied all the best paintings, and then came home and toiled day and night in mixing, and applying colors so attentively to the canvas?"

He replied, "I am painting for eternity."

Oh! could every parent, teacher, and minister understand this statement of the Artist! But his picture from the long years of study, toil, and suffering; what is it, compared with your child?

Yet, Raphael could spend a life-time and a world of treasure on it! And Michael Angelo could exhaust all his powers and the income of a nation to finish that picture.

Cannot you spend a few years to educate that child? Cannot you give your influence and income to have and aid an intensely anxious and vital ministry, and leave a few pictures in the galleries of that child's memory and spirit that will inspire many a lost one from sin and death, to redemption and peace, and so leave your name where it will never die?

Plutarch give us a learned Dissertation on the single Greek word " ετ " found inscribed on the Temple of Appollo at Delphi. In the *Ionic dialect* we are told that it means — " I wish." This perfectly expressed the state of mind of all who entered the temple on the business of consultation. And an ancient scholar of great worth assumes that it is the initial word of a celebrated line in the 3d book of the Odyssey, and stands there as signifying the whole line which is thus rendered, viz: — " Oh that the gods would empower me to obtain my wishes!"

Oh! that there was some such *initial* word in our mother tongue, that could be inscribed over every church-door; the rendering of which should be this, viz: — " Oh! that God would empower me to obtain my wishes for my child!"

But further. Back of all this needed culture, and around it, lays the purpose and effort, the will and energy and learning of the clergy. And for years, as a town's committee, Mr. Ainsworth held the school teachers in his hand; and who shall say today, how much of our life, capability, integrity and prudence, energy, and will-power, eminated from that noble and heroic minister? I may be presumptuous, but I firmly believe that the clergy who are in this world, not to be ministered unto but to minister, hold a position to which there is no other paramount. And to stimulate you up to its importance, worth and influence, I will enterrogate you. — Where in barbary and in a servitude worse then was Southern Slavery would be woman's condition, if the christian ministry had never existed? — If it had never existed, where would be our homes and children, and our hopes of the life to come? — Without the Christian ministry, how conceive and support a free and enlightened government? — without the ministry of the divine Word, how would you make, mould and educate its legislators and judges?

You study this subject, and it will be seen that our government — the best this side of heaven and founded on God's impartial rule, could not carry out its principles,—could not secure life, liberty, and the pursuit of happiness to man, without the ministry — the preaching of the Gospel. Without the christian Clergy men could not be qualified to respect constituted authorities and administer laws. Without the ministry, man is not capable of self-government. Without the ministry of the Gospel, Kingdoms and nations could not be kept from the inroads of passion, taint, corruption and ruin. Sodom, and Gomorah, Ninevah and Babylon, Egypt and Jerusalem, Greece, Carthage and Rome, attest with overwhelming evidence the awful consequences, in their complete destruction, of rejecting the ministry of patriarchs, and prophets, of Christ and the Apostles.

Thus we see that the richest, proudest, and most cultivated nations, with all their forts and navies, with all their schools, arts and sciences, have been swept from the face of the earth, because they refused the preaching of the great and good who were sent unto them. Remove a nation's honor, justice and virtue, which are the results of preaching and sanctuary privileges, and you take away every band that can hold her together, and remove all the elements of her life.

A christian Clergy educate into society, all her convictions and understandings of moral obligations and accountability. They lift men to clear conceptions of duty to themselves, to those around them and to God; and thus hold society in compact and contract. The christian Clergy are the conquering and aggressive forces on infidelity, and the absorbing army of all idoliatry and its baleful effects. The gospel ministry imparts the needed means, and grace required by all men to escape death and acquire life, to pass from the ruins and woes of earth to the orders and joys of blessed character. Preaching bears away our iniquity, absorbs all sin and evil, cleanses the spirit, renews

the affections ; bears all men from darkness to light, and makes
man at-one-ment with God. Through ministering, Christ made
his disciples the light of the world. And the Clergy have borne
on that light which lighteth every man that cometh, and which is
pressing every person with the necessity of repentance and re-
generation. They aid, increase, and vitalize the information
about the resurrection, which inspires all men to a higher life.
The gospel ministry imparts the light and truth and intuition,
which cannot be read from books, cannot be discovered in the
best composition, cannot be rendered by the ablest stenographer,
cannot be written by the most versatile genius possessed with
the most copious vocabulary. Never forget then, that it was the
living soul in what Demothenes said, that moved the Athenians ;
it was the immortal spirit in the utterances of Cicero, that thril-
led the Senate ; it was the flashing of undying light in the eye
and mien of Patrick Henry that held our Fathers spell-bound at
the birth of Liberty ; it was the soul of Paul in the intense, concentrated, and burning truths, flashing out and shimmering in
lines of fire, by which the great Apostle entranced the wisdom
and learning of Rome and Athens ! And it is the eye, and the
spirit, and the light of the clergy which are required to combine
and concen trate, and intensify the doctrines, the precepts, and
examples of Christ until you are swept into purity, into sympho-
ny with peace, with spiritual passion and power, and the ener-
gies of everlasting life.

In such an hour of endless impressions, souls are born, affections renewed, hearts regenerated, and all of society moves up
from barbarism to God and Christ. In such an hour the Clergyman is no longer a *preacher* merely, but humanity itself, — tram-
pled, torn, bleeding, yet beautiful, — starting one glorious moment in her terrible ruin, with her hand lifted to the blue heavens over her heroic DEAD, and affirming her Great Oath, in the
elemental life that is Christ to live.

I would bear to you at last then, in the urn of remembrance,
ashes from the fires of the wondrous dead, to intensify your
sense of the importance and worth of the christian clergy of the
past and of today.

May you work *for* and *with* them as you would wish to have done when you look back on earth and the loved ones you leave behind, then will you receive in some measure the glorious answer of life's great prayer. And when you come to the congregation of silence, —

They, who stand around your grave,
Will rank you nobly.

SENTIMENT No. 11. — "Jaffrey — Her Past and Her Present." Response by Dr. Daniel B. Cutter, of Peterboro', N. H.

Mr. President: — It affords me great pleasure to meet you and my former associates, here today. Few indeed are our numbers, so few, that in this vast congregation here assembled, I recognize only here and there a familiar face. Time has made such sad inroad into our numbers, that today I feel like a stranger in my own native town. The old Church, the place where our fathers worshiped, in gone by days, now stands a memorial of its former greatness, but the sound of the gospel is there no longer heard. Minister and people lie buried together in yonder grave-yard, silent in the sleep of death. For ever sacred be their ashes. To commemorate the doings of these men is the occasion of our meeting here today. A little more than 100 years ago, the place, on which we now stand, and its surrounding as far as the eye can reach, was an unbroken forest. On the banks of the Contoocook grew the lofty pine, while on the hills and in the valleys grew a variety of hard wood, fir and hemlock; the mountain, which now presents a bare rock, was covered with spruce. From its side flowed numerous rippling streams, which, after passing through bog and swamp, united their flowing waters and formed the Contoocook river. The inhabitants of this, then wild domain, was the moose, the deer, the bear and the wolf, together with the wild turkey and the partridge. The streams were filled with trout, and the ponds with pickerel. Over this wild domain, in majestic grandeur, then clad with fir, now bald with age, peered the lofty Monadnock, surveying the vast territory around, watching the progress of events, as the white man, here and there, made inroads in his wild domain. Such was Jaffrey, when in 1752, Moses Stickney, Richard Peabody, and seven others, made an attempt at settlement in the Southeast part of the town. Through fear of the Indians, they all soon left except one of their number, known as Capt. Platts. During their stay, on Dec. 9th, 1753, Moses Stickney had a son born, whose name was Simon, who is supposed to be the first white child born in Jaffrey. He never after resided there, but returned with his father to Boxford, Mass., and on maturity, settled in Holden, and afterwards removed to New Haven, Vt., and died in 1791. He left three daughters.

The next attempt at settlement was made by a colony of hardy adventurers from Londonderry, encouraged probably by their brethren, who had previously made a settlement in Peterboro', an adjoining township. But few of these however had the hardihood to remain as permanent settlers. After enduring the hardships and privations of a pioneer life for a time, they sold their rights to a Massachusetts colony, mostly from Essex and Middlesex Counties. These were the men, who on the 14th of September 1773, met and organized the town. This was done by virtue of a charter granted by his Excellency, John Wentworth, then Governor of the Province of New Hampshire, and Council, at Portsmouth, August 17th, 1773, who changed the original name, *Middle Monadnock No. 2*, to Jaffrey, in honor of George Jaffrey, Esq., one of the original proprietors. The first town meeting was held at the house of Francis Wright, Innkeeper, situated on Lot No. 14, Range 8. A second meeting was held at the same place, on the 28th of the same month, and £80 L. M. was voted for the repairing of roads, and £6 L. M. for preaching. No church was then built. They had preaching probably, in some private house. The next year, 1774, the town voted to build a meeting-house. Voted to raise said house in June, 1775. This was the first year of the Revolutionary War, one battle had already been fought, another was pending ; 16 of their men were in the field, and while raising the church, it is said, the sound of the cannon was heard from Bunker Hill. Actuated by a sense of duty, they did not despond, but readily obeyed the call of their Country : men, money, provisions, and munitions of war, were promptly furnished, and when we learn that a town of only 351 inhabitants furnished 72 men during the war, we cannot be surprised at their success in that war.

During seven long and perilous years, they met the requirments of their country, and through the blessing of God, triumphed at last, and laid the foundation of her future greatness. We, their descendants, may well feel proud of such fathers, and mothers too, who, if they were not in the battle field, were in other fields, doing no less glorious service for their God, and their country. During all this period of war and suffering, the church was not only raised, but so far completed as to be made use of for public worship. With the men of that time, a neglect of religious duty would have been fatal, in their minds, to their success in battle. They relied on the God of heaven, and acted under a sense of His presence, feeling sure of victory only through His aid and with His blessing.

In 1780 a church was organized, and on December 10, 1782, the Rev. Laban Ainsworth was ordained their pastor; who, during an extraordinary long life, administered to the wants of this people, in all matters pertaining to religious duty. In person he was of medium height, in appearance dignified, in deportment affable, which together with an intellectual superiority, enabled him to command the love and respect of his fellow men. He was the ruling power of the church, the district school, and I might say, the town. For a long series of years he was the Superintending School Committee, whose frequent visits and sage counsel I well remember. In the early days of the town, the education of their children was a matter of interest. In 1775, £8 lawful money was voted for a school. No schoolhouses were then built. Where the school was taught is a matter of conjecture. School-houses, school-teachers and schoolbooks were rare things in those days. The Bible, the psalmbook and the primer were almost the only books in their possession. With such means, it must have required the ingenuity of a mother to teach their children to read.

The Spelling-book, Reader and Arithmetic at length made their appearance. With a determination admirable, and patience remarkable, they overcame every obstacle, established schools, educated their children, furnished the world with 25

College Graduates, besides many more who qualified themselves for a professional life by an Academical education. Jaffrey has furnished Pastors for the Church, Counselors for the Bar, and Physicians for the sick. One of her sons, has been honored with the seat of Chief Justice in his own State, while another is a distinguished Missionary in Ceylon.

The clouds of war at length pass away;—the sushine of peace blesses the land. The farmer returns to the plough, the mechanic to his work-shop, the merchant to his counter, the swords are beat into ploughshares, and bayonets into reaping hooks, and the people hope to learn war no more.

A new era has now commenced; the foot-paths gradually become passable roads; the rude cabin a framed house; the thatched hovel a commodious barn; the forest falls, upon its ashes the fertile field and the green meadows appear. The little school-house is seen here and there, by the side of the road. Grist-mills, saw-mills, stores and taverns—showing trade and travel—are now becoming common. Wheel carriages take the place of the saddle and the pillion,—the whole family can now ride to church. The turnpike, the wonder of the age, is now built, opening the way for a stage coach from Boston to Wapole and back, twice a week, which in its turn, affords not only means of conveyance for passengers, but for a mail also, which is established, and a Post Office too; letters can now be sent and received. The sons and daughters abroad, can exchange letters with their parents at home, and to cap the climax, they can now take a Newspaper, one being published at Keene, in 1799.

The town is now in a healthy, thriving condition, all of the necessaries and conveniences of life are at command. The farmer can now sleep undisturbed by the howl of the wolf, prowling around for the destruction of his flock,—his herd and flock are safe in the field by night as well as by day,—no more herding or folding necessary. He is indeed lord of his own domain, independent of all monopolies.

We have now reached the present century, the age of scientific research, the age of invention, the age of high intellectual culture and refinement. The winds and the waves now obey

the dictate of man, and are made subservient to his wishes.
The lighning too at his command, carries intelligence at his bid-
ding.   Head work is the order of the day, and bodily labor dis-
creditable.   No means are spared in the culture of the intellect,
and hardly any used for the improvement of the moral and physical organization.   Greatness has left the seat of goodness, and
now sits in the lap of ease and luxury.   We are now showered
with blessings, but like Rome of old, are we not in danger of the
Goths and Vandals?   Will not the extravagance of our times,
so destructive to our offspring, open wide the door for the en-
trance of another race that will supplant us?   Or do we look
forward, with the expectation of Abraham of old, that our children and our children's children are to be the possessors of this
gift of their fathers, through all coming generations? Do we rely
on our intelligence? so did Rome on her's.   Do we rely on our
own goodness? so did the children of Abraham on their's.   Both
fell!   By obeying the precepts of the Lord, our fathers were
blessed, and we, their descendants, can receive the same blessing,
only by the same obedience.   May we then emulate their virtues, and render due obedience to the precepts of our Heavenly
Father.

SENTIMENT No. 12. — " The Homes of Our Youth." Response by Rev. Andrew O. Warren, of Montrose, Pa.

Mr. President, Ladies and Gentlemen ; Fellow Townsmen : —
I do not come forward to make a speech at this hour, for I have
none written.   But I did think this morning that possibly I
might find one here already written at my hands.   If I were to
speak at all, you would find that I was good in dispersing a
crowd in that way.

But allow me to congratulate you, fellow townsmen, at this
time, for the grand history of the past 100 years that is closed
by this anniversary, and for its grander prophecy for the next
century.

I feel it to be one of the proudest days of my life, that I am
permitted to be here and to acknowledge this as my native place.
Here indeed are " the dear homes of our youth."   Here we began our very being and laid the foundation for every superstruct-

ure, — we have our record, morally, socially, intellectually and spiritually. My native place was in School District No. 4, and I hope I never have, nor shall be permitted to dishonor it. Well do I remember some of the old people in that section of the town, particularly one old Mr. Horton, who was favored far above the most of his neighbors by the Divine Being if we can believe his story. He said as he was working by his flat piece, the voice of the Lord came to him and said, "go preach my word to the people." At first he excused himself, but on the repetition of the call, he started out. Came to my father's house and talked to my good mother day after day. One Sunday he made an appointment at the school-house and I attended. During his speech he said he should preach nothing that was not found between the lids of the Bible. But he soon began a tirade of abuse upon the " pocky cotton factories," and other corporations in the land, and declared his conviction that they would be the ruin of our country. But the country lives, —the cotton mills live and prosper, but Mr. Horton rests with his fathers.

I remember particularly my first Sunday school-teacher. Levi Fisk, Esq., and I never shall forget one remark made by him. He was a man of good judgment in most matters, yet he had his weak points. Speaking of Railroads, as one was then being talked of from Boston to Bellows Falls, one route might lay across some part of our town ; the old squire " said he would rather have three of the best farm buildings in town all destroyed by fire annually, to be replaced by taxes on the town, rather than have a Railroad in it." You of this hour do not concur in that opinion. If it were to be said now, no more cars would ever enter your town, you would seek and follow the cars wherever they went.

But I will not detain you. From "the homes of our youth," . many of us have made a wide departure. Yet it is no matter where we may go in after time, we shall find no place around which cluster such hallowed memories as gather here. In memory we see again the forms of our fathers and mothers, long since gone to their eternal rest, gliding in our midst. We hear their voices saying to us here, we lived, toiled and died to sow the seeds, the fruit of which, you, our children, are permitted this day to gather.

Mighty changes have marked the march of years that are past, but the record is good. Go forward still, with a stout heart and manly purpose, and you shall have a grander history to conclude 100 years from today. Not one of us shall see that distant time, save in promise, the reality of which we cannot doubt.

The whole field of my thought at this time is beautifully expressed by the poet, if I am able to call the words to mind, thus:

Life is like a stately temple
  That is founded in the sea,
Whose uprising fair proportions
  Penetrate immensity;
Love the architect who builds it,
  Building it eternally.

Tome, standing in the present,
  As one waits beside a grave,
Up the isles and to the altar
  Rolls the Past its solemn wave,
With a murmer as of mourning,
  Undulating in the nave.

Pallid phantoms glide around me
  In the wrecks of hope and home;
Voices moan among the waters,
  Faces vanish in the foam;
But a peace, divine, unfailing,
  Writes its promise in the dome.

Cold the waters where my feet are,
  But my heart is strung anew,
Tuned to Hope's profound vibration,
Pulsing all the ether through,
For the seeking souls that ripen
  In a patience strong and true.

Hark! the all-inspiring Angel
  Of the Future leads the choir;
All the shadows of the temple
  Are illumed with living lire,
And the bells above are waking
  Chimes of infinite desire.

For the strongest or the weakest
  There is no eternal fall;
Many graves and many mourners,
  But at last — the lifted pall!
For the highest and the lowest
  Blessed life containeth all.

O thou fair unfinished temple!
  In unfathomed sea begun,
Love, thy builder, shapes and lifts thee
  In the glory of the sun;
And the builder and the builded
  To the pure in heart — are one.

PARTING HYMN.

BY MISS HENRIETTA S. CUTTER.

AIR — "*Auld Lang Syne.*"

The Band, Choir and audience unitedly swelling " the tide of song along.'

The shades of night are gathering fast,
Round old Monadnock's brow,
While we must say the parting word,
With friendship's hand clasp now ;
While we must break the golden links
That bind reunion's chain
Yet often memory 'll bear us back—
Back to this day again.

Among the many gathered here
Are those of sterling worth,
Upon whose brows the impress rests
Of the great and good of earth ;
And with those passing down life's hill,
Just coming up are some,
Whose laurel crown for worthy deeds
In th' future must be won.

'Mid joys of this Centennial day,
A silent tear we shed,
For parents, brothers, sisters, friends,
Now sleeping with the dead
They 've left to us the well-worn paths
On life's great harvest field ;
May we the seed full early sow,
That th' grain may heavy yield.

One century hence — that future day
Is only known to God ;
But WE shall rest all peacefully
Beneath the flowering sod.
We 've met today, and now we part —
Now we must say " good-bye ;"
May Heaven's rich blessings on all rest —
We 'll meet again on high.

Peter Upton, Esq. moved that this meeting adjourn for one hundred years, and it was unanimously voted. Three cheers for " The One Hundredth Anniversary of the Town of Jaffrey " preceded a quiet dispersal of home-seeking strangers and townspeople from the soon deserted canvass.

NOTE.—We are indebted to George Wilder Fox for a portion of this, (copied), as reported by him for the New Hampshire Sentinel.

The following letters were received from the absent sons of Jaffrey, who could not, for reasons therein specified, unite in the centennial exercises.

PITTSBURGH, PA , JULY 23, 1873.

To Julius Cutter and Others, Committee :

GENTLEMEN :—I have the honor to acknowledge the receipt of your letter inviting me to be present at the Centennial Anniversary of the incorporation of the town of Jaffrey. It would give me great pleasure to be there on an occasion of such interest to all natives of the dear old town ; but the state of my health will not permit it. Wherever its sons and daughters may wander, or wherever dwell, their thoughts must frequently turn back with kindly regards, as mine do, to the home of childhood : and we are always glad to know that the friends we left behind us there still enjoy the thrift and comforts that come by industry and skill, in the useful arts.   God bless old Jaffrey, and its people.

Situated near the geographical centre of New England, that town well represents New England character and life; and its granite hills and towering mountain as well represent the old *Granite State.*   It is *New England* in its purity; and its character is strongly impressed upon its children.   Wherever we may be, we are Americans and patriots; attached to the homes of our adoption; but *Yankees* still.

A *Century* is a long time.   Yet the first settled minister of the town lived in honor and esteem to see his centennial birthday.   But how many events have occurred in that time!   A Century ago considerable portions of the thirty Indian tribes that once inhabited New England, were still within its borders.   Now, none remain: and even their languages are all dead, or exist only on the silent pages of the Eliot Bible.   A wide region has become a fruitful land, distinguished for industry and intelligence, and out from among you have gone very many, to people new regions towards the setting sun.

A Century hence, let Jaffrey again call together her children, and out from among a hundred and fifty millions people, stretching quite across a continent, they will come; and will rejoice to find old Jaffrey still prosperous and happy.

Wishing you a large and pleasant meeting,

I am, Yours very truly,

GEO. F. GILLMORE.

OBERLIN, OHIO, AUGUST 15, 1873.

F. H. Cutter, and Others:

DEAR SIRS:—The card of invitation to the Jaffrey Centennial was duly received.   I do not know of anything that would give me more pleasure than to attend this celebration, if I could afford the journey.   Jaffrey is my birth-place, and the birth-place of my mother, and all my brothers and sisters but one.   It is just a third of a century since my father, with nine children, removed to this place.   With us came my father's father, and a brother and sister of my mother,—Thomas and Betsey Joslin.   Of the fourteen, only my mother and three younger sisters and myself remain.

I have repeatedly visited Jaffrey, and renewed the impressions of early boyhood.   There is no spot on earth so full of interesting associations and touching memories, as that mountain town. Every object, from the cloud capped Monadnock, to the old school-house and blacksmith shop at the middle of the town, is full of suggestions and tender interest. The very changeless- ness of the upper part of the town, is a gratification. It still stands as it appeared to my nine years old eyes, a third of a century ago; and I can but hope that it will remain so. I should delight to bring the greetings of my mother and our family to the friends of our childhood, and join in celebrating the birthday of the dear old town. If she is poor in soil, she is rich in the beauty and grandeur of her scenery, and rich in her children and grand-children, scattered over all the land. May your commem- oration be one worthy of the venerable mothers, and a satisfac- tion to all the sons and daughters who may gather from near and far. If any printed record is prepared, please send two or three copies to me, with my share of the expense.

Yours truly,

JOHN M. ELLIS.

CANANDAIGUA, MICHIGAN, AUG. 14, 1873.

Jaffrey Centennial Committee of Arrangements:

GENTLEMEN:—Your kind invitation for me to be present at the Centennial gathering of my native town, reached me in due time. It would give me great pleasure to be with you on that occasion; to meet friends from whom I have been long separated, and whom I may never see elsewhere. But my present surroundings and duties will compel me to decline your invitation and remain at home. If tradition be not at fault, it is just one hundred years since my grand-father, Phineas Spaulding, in the Southwest part of the town, broke the forest that after- wards made him a pleasant home. Then, the only highway was a footpath through the tangled wildwood, and trees that had been marked and scathed by the woodman's axe or hatchet; the only guide to those denizens of the forest, from one point to an- other,—to meeting and to mill. Then, too, the slow footed ox, yoked and hitched to the old two-wheeled cart in summer, and the heavy sled in winter, was the only pleasure carriage for week-day or for Sunday, and the only mode of conveyance from neighbor to neighbor, or from town to town. Horses were few, and mostly used for riding on the back. It was no uncommon thing for man and wife to be seen riding both on one beast; he in front on the saddle and she behind on the pillion. Young ladies with their beaux would thus ride for recreation and for pleasure, till the pillion gave place for another horse and side-saddle, and then they traveled side by side. Sixty years ago, on the spot now occupied by your commodious Hotel, stood the dwelling-house of Dea. Eleazer Spofford, which, with outbuild-ings, and grist and saw mill down by the river, were about all that could be seen for buildings, where your pleasant village now stands. Spofford's mills were known for their superiority of workmanship over everything else of the kind, for many miles around. One little anecdote as touching the old saw mill I can remember in my boyhood days.

When it was first in operation, as one gate shut and another opened, moving the heavy carriage with its ponderous log to and from the saw, a colored man standing by in amazement, ex-claimed: " Massa Spofford, don't you think you could invent a machine to hoe corn ? "

Those were primitive days; times when our grand-fathers and grand-mothers had to toil for their daily food, and right glad were they, if they could bring the two ends of the year to meet, with a few spare dollars for deposit against the time of need.— In those early days, almost every house held its instrument—not the modern piano, but the old fashioned spinning wheel, and while the foot pressed the pedal, the fingers instead of gliding over keys of ivory to the tune of Yankee Doodle, or God save the King, or perchance the more solemn strains of Old Hundred or St′ Martyn's, were busy in drawing the thread from the pine distaff, to be wrought into cloth for the clothing of the house-hold. I will venture the assertion that you cannot in your town today, find a young lady under twenty years of age, that can spin a skein of fine linen, or in her grand-mother's old hand loom weave a yard of cloth. I say this, not by way of disparagement to any one, for I well know that modern improvements and ma-chinery have done away with most of that kind of labor. To-day you have your pleasant homes, your good roads, your car-riages of comfort and of ease, and instead of the lumbering stage coach that used daily to pass through your village, from Keene to Boston, is seen the iron horse, puffing and blowing on his feed of fire, and drawing in his wake a burden that many stage teams could not move an inch.

I have hastily gleaned at a few things in the century that has passed, but who among your gathering today will be present to read the history of the century to come ? It would be no pre-sumption to answer *not one.*

In conclusion, I will offer the following sentiment: "Old Jaffrey:—May her virtue and mora'ity keep even pace with her internal improvements for a hundred years to come."

Very respectfully yours,

LYMAN SPAULDING.

BARRE, VT., AUGUST 18, 1873.

Mr. Julius Cutter:

MY DEAR SIR:—Ever since the reception of your invitation to be present and participate in the celebration of the Centennial Anniversary of the incorporation of the town, I have hoped to meet you there. But the debility from which I am just now suffering, reminds me that quiet is better suited to my condition.

You may know that during ten years and a half I was engaged in examining the teachers and caring for the children of your Common Schools, I knew all the young people of school-age; and, before I left town, I copied all their names and ages from the registers. Were it permitted, I should like to respond to the sentiment, " Our Common Schools." We have been nurtured there, and we are all the alumni or alumnæ of that institution. You meet as graduates from the people's college.— Though you differ in your religions and political preferences, here you are brethren.

The early inhabitants of Jaffrey so recognized the necessity of schools, that, ninety-eight years ago last April, at the second annual town meeting that was holden under the charter, an appropriation of eight pounds was voted for the support of a school. Ever since that time, it is known that the town has every year, except one, voted a sum of money for a like purpose. The first school-house was built at the expense of the town, in the year 1778. It stood just across the road from father Ainsworth's house, and remained there till the year 1809. Within twelve years after this first house was put up, there were nine others in town.

Could you examine a catalogue which contained the names of all who have shared in the advantages of your schools, and could you read their history also, you would see a record of which you might justly be proud.

I remain, Very truly yours,

LEONARD TENNEY.

AMHERST, JULY 18, 1873.

DEAR SIR:—Yours of the 28th ult. giving me notice of the Centennial Celebration at Jaffrey, on the 20th prox. and of a sentiment to which I am invited to respond, has been received.

I have delayed answering hoping to be able to so arrange my business engagements, that I might be present on that occasion, but I find it will not be possible for me to attend. I have an engagement which takes me to Chicago, at that time, which cannot be postponed. I regret very much that I cannot have the pleasure of meeting the good citizens of my native town on that day, and enjoying the festivities of the occasion, but my time being previously engaged, is not at my own disposal.

Wishing you a successful and pleasant Celebration on the day appointed, I am,

Very truly, your obedient servant,

E. S. CUTTER.

F. H. Cutter, Esq., Jaffrey, N. H.

YATES CITY, KNOX COUNTY, ILLINOIS, AUG. 8, 1873.

To the Committee of Arrangements:

DEAR SIRS:—Your kind favor, inviting me to be present with you upon the occasion of your Centennial, has been received. but it finds me engrossed in business arrangements, such that I cannot conveniently accept your invitation; a privilege which I should most dearly love to enjoy.— This being the case, I trust you will allow me to express a thought that seems full in my mind, and thus add my mite to your festivities.

More than twenty-five years have passed since I broke bands with the dear old town and friends, and launched out upon the unknown future to pursue my journey through life; yet I have not forgotten the spot that gave me birth. The broad prairies and boundless harvests, fill my soul with gladness and my heart with thanksgiving, but my mind continually runs back with delight to my old native New Hampshire hills, with Jaffrey for its centre, and the gray old Monadnock for its chief corner stone.

Oh Memory! What volumes fill thy space as I contemplate the past. I live over again the days of my youth; I think of the sports of No. 11; of the achievements in "Melville;" I wonder at my efforts in No. 6, and feel surprised at my success in No. 3; I contemplate the pleasures of our social and religious privileges; our lyceum and singing schools; our annual trainings and musters and 4th of July celebrations, and wonder if it took them all to help make me a man? Aye, and I answer to myself, yes! and more too, for it requires the determination to be a man. In the days of the Cæsars, it was the height of ambition to become a Roman citizen. How much more for every one born upon American soil, to be in truth an American citizen.— Reflecting upon the efforts that were made use of to fit us who are upon the present drama of life, by our fathers and mothers who have mostly gone to their reward, let it remind us of our duty to those whom Providence has placed in our charge, the young of the land.

Honored as old Jaffrey has always been for the virtue and general intelligence of its citizens, with how much pleasure can you turn to your young and youth and feel that a brighter future is before them than we enjoy. The generous munificence of one of your townsmen, has placed greater privileges and brighter prospects before you, and as the town has so far already honored itself, what may not the most sanguine expect hereafter?

The sun never shone upon lovelier hills; man was never fanned by purer breezes; streams never rattled down precipices freer than do those in your own, *my own* native town. The arts and sciences lend their aid, and your old men and your old women, your young men and your young women, yes, and your youth, may, if they will, be honored and praised throughout the land.

Permit me then, to close by offering this sentiment: "The good old town of Jaffrey; Wherever her sons or daughters rove, may her memory to them be as bright as her waters are pure and their honor as lasting as Monadnock itself."

Yours with much respect,

D. COREY, JR.

CAMPTONVILLE, N. H., AUG. 15th, 1873.

Gentlemen of the Committee:

Your invitation to attend the Centennial Celebration at Jaffrey, on the 20th inst., has been received. I regret that engagements at home will prevent my attendance upon that interesting occasion.

Though not a native of Jaffrey, I went there to reside at so early a period of my life, that whatever is pleasant in youthful recollections of home and early friends are centered there.

My acquaintances with Jaffrey commenced in that transition period when it was changing from an almost exclusively agricultural town, to one of manufacturing and educational facilities as well.

The early fathers of the town, such as the first Col. Prescott, the first Dr. Howe, Judge Parker, Capt. Joseph Cutter, John Cutter, tanner, I remember as silver haired men at that time, who soon passed away, and gave place to their descendants of the second generation, who worthily carried forward the town in its career of prosperity and literary advancement. To men of this generation the town was indebted for the establishment of Melville Academy, an institution which exerted an extensive and abiding influence for good, and carries to a high degree the standard of education among the sons and daughters of Jaffrey. And, although this institution has ceased to exist, it is a matter of congratulation that the munificence of one of her citizens has continued to Jaffrey the means of a good High School education to all her youth in the future.

I have been pleased to note in occasional visits, the rapid progress of Jaffrey in material prosperity, and hope she may continue in her onward march of improvement.

In conclusion, I would say that I have dwelt for a time in the far South, where the Orange blooms, and the Fig and the Pomegranate put forth leaves and fruit; I have resided in the middle region of our Country, where the Grape and the Peach and the Nectarine flourish, I have traveled Westward to the centre of that great valley where the Mississippi rolls its vast volume of waters, where waving fields of grain furnish food for a continent, but I have yet to see the land which on the whole, the dwellers round the base of the Monadnock, need envy its possesion as a home.

With best wishes to the Committee personally, and hope that an auspicious day may render the Celebration a success,

I remain, yours very truly,

CHARLES CUTTER.

To F. H. Cutter and others.

MANSFIELD, OHIO, AUG. 11, 1873.

Committee of Arrangements ; — GENTLEMEN :—I received your card of invitation to attend a Celebration of the One Hundredth Anniversary of the Incorporation of the Town of Jaffrey.

Living in what was called the *far West* when I left my New Hampshire home, I can only send my regrets at not being able to be present on that interesting occasion, and visit

> The land where a father dwells,
> And that holds a mother's grave.

My mind reverts to many scenes of youthful days, since receiving your card. I often think of the daily labor of New England Farmers' boys, who, from my experience, go into the field at an early age, and get permission to go fishing only when it rains too hard to work out of doors, and there is no corn to shell. This, with brown bread and milk for supper, gives a boy a good constitution with which to fight the battle of life.

I often think of the days, when, for the want of something to read, I walked four miles to the old church to attend the Sabbath School, get a Library book, and hear the good old man preach, who then dressed in the fashion of our revolutionary fathers. On my last visit to Jaffrey, I was glad to see that ancient edifice in so good a state of preservation. May it stand another century, a monument to religion, morality and education.

During the late strife for the preservation of our glorious Union, there was talk, even in Ohio, of our Country being divided — the East from the West, as well as the North from the South. I thought of my admiration of the great West, the country of my adoption, and my love for New England, the land of my nativity, and often found myself repeating a verse I had cut from some paper about the time of leaving my native State, which I will offer as a sentiment ;

> "New England, dear New England,
> My birth-place proud and free ;
> A traitor's curse be on my head,
> When I am false to thee."

Please remember me kindly to all the friends of my youth, in in the good old Town of Jaffrey.

Very truly yours,

P. BIGELOW.

CAMBRIDGE, AUGUST, 1873.

DEAR SIR:— I thank you for the invitation to your Centennial festival. If my health would have permitted, it would have given me much pleasure to have joined in the celebration. I have been told that I was born in Jaffrey, but it was so long ago, 1784, that none of the present inhabitants could testify to the fact; but as it would be equally difficult to produce any evidence to the contrary, I may as well, on this occasion, claim the honor. I understand that my parents removed from Jaffrey to New Ipswich when I was about a year old, and the most that I recollect of Jaffrey, relates to my being sent there to school, about seventy-eight years ago. The school was kept by a foreigner, by the name of Dillon, who had a great reputation for teaching penmanship, and was about as much celebrated for the use of the rod as the pen, and I dare say tradition may have preserved some anecdotes of his severe teachings in that line, which were of a nature to be remembered as long as any of his other lessons. At this school I was a class-mate with General James Miller, who got his education rather late in life, and we studied our English Grammar together, in the same seat, he at the age of twenty-one, and I at the age of eleven. I think Dillon never attempted to use the rod upon Miller; if he had, the future warrior might have commenced his campaign some years before the war of 1812. Among the school-mates that I remember, were Dr. Abner Howe and his brother Dr. Adonijah Howe, who are, no doubt, well remembered and much respected by many of the present inhabitants of Jaffrey. Andrew Thorndike was one of the familiar names of that day, though considerably older than my school-mates.

Some years after my school boy days, I recollect climbing to the top of Monadnock, and finding on the highest pinnacle, a date, and what appeared to be the initial letter of three or four names, rudely pounded out, with much labor, on the solid ledge apparently by the use of no better implement than a stone. This may probably still be found there, though not without careful search, as the inscription though deep is rather indistinct. It may probably be a record of the first visit to the mountain after the settlement of the country, and would be a very interesting item in the history of your Centennial, if it had not already been published. I took a copy of it at the time, but have not been able to find it.

With best wishes for the continuance of the prosperity of my native town.

Your humble servant,

L. L. PIERCE. ESQ.   SAMUEL BATCHELDER.

The following is a list of the names of those who subscribed to pay the expenses of the Centennial Celebration, with the amount paid by each.

John Fox,	$25 00	William P. Stevens,	2 00
Gurley A. Phelps,	1 00	Charles Stevens,	3 00
Ethan Cutter,	5 00	Henry Chamberlain,	3 00
Joseph P. Frost,	5 00	Anson W. Jewett,	5 00
Asa Nutting,	3 00	Gustavus A. Cutter,	3 00
Timothy Blodgett,	10 00	John S. Dutton,	3 00
Laban Rice,	5 00	Frederic Spaulding,	5 00
Jonas C. Rice,	10 00	Otis G. Rice,	5 00
Edwin R. Cutter,	5 00	Levi E. Brigham,	3 00
Benjamin F. Lawrence,	10 00	Jonathan J. Comstock,	3 00
Geo. F. Potter,	1 00	I. E. Keeys,	1 00
Edmund C. Shattuck,	2 00	Ambrose W. Spaulding,	5 00
Thomas K. Goff,	1 00	J. F. Stone,	1 00
Lucius A. Cutter,	5 00	Daniel P. Adams,	5 00
Nathaniel Cutter,	5 00	Addison J. Adams,	3 00
Julius Cutter,	15 00	E. G. Bryant,	2 00
Jonathan D. Gibbs,	1 00	Jonas Cutter,	10 00
Luke French,	1 00	Joseph T. Bigelow,	5 00
Rufus Case,	4 00	Richard Spaulding,	5 00
John A. Cutter,	10 00	Vryling D. Shattuck,	2 00
Lyman K. Farnum,	1 00	Austin A. Spaulding,	1 00
Eleazer W. Heath,	2 00	Michael D. Fitzgerald,	5 00
Charles A. Baldwin,	1 00	Leonard E. Spaulding,	2 00
Charles C. Libby,	1 00	Clarrence S. Bailey,	3 00
George F. Gilmore,	1 00	Lafayett Blood,	3 00
John Conant,	20 00	Marshall C. Adams,	3 00
Arad Adams,	10 00	John S. Lawrence,	5 00
Franklin H. Cutter,	15 00	Peter Hogan,	1 00
John W. Woodruff,	2 00	Francis Lowe,	1 00
Nehemiah Cutter,	4 00	Benjamin Cutter,	20 00
James R. Harrington,	1 00	Joseph Davis, .	2 00
Edmund P. Shattuck,	5 00	C. B. Davis,	1 00
Henry C. French,	5 00	Dexter Pierce,	1 00
Joseph W. Fassett,	5 00	Charles Bacon,	2 00
Geo. A. Underwood,	15 00	Joseph A. Thayer,	1 00
Ezra Baker,	5 00	Luke Nutting,	1 00
Milton Baker,	5 00	Benjamin L. Baldwin,	2 00
John Hecker,	5 00	Levi Pollard,	1 00
Levi P. Towne,	3 00	William Upton,	1 00
Charles A. Cutter,	2 00	Samuel T. Wellman,	5 00

Stephen F. Bacon,	1 00	John M. Wales,	2 00
Luke Carter,	1 00	Albert Bass,	2 00
Elijah Smith,	2 00	Miss A. Parker,	2 00
John Frost,	3 00	Peter Upton,	5 00
Isaac S. Russell,	5 00	Mrs. S. H. Rand,	2 00
Samuel Hodge,	1 00	Leonard F. Sawyer,	2 00
Benjamin F. Prescott,	1 00	Edward Cary,	1 00
John Perry,	3 00	Josiah M. M. Lacy,	2 00
Thomas A. Stearns,	5 00	Miss Rebecca Bacon,	2 00
Addison Pierce,	2 00	Cummings Sawyer,	2 00
Samuel Marble,	2 00	E. H. Tower,	2 00
Oren Prescott,	2 00	Mrs. E. C. Duncan,	10 00
Joseph Joslin,	5 00	Oliver Bacon,	1 00
T. H. Curtis,	5 00	Charles L. Clark,	2 00
Robert Ritchie,	5 00	Jonathan Page,	2 00
Samuel Ryan,	5 00	Charles E. Cutter,	5 00
Charles H. Powers,	5 00	Alvah Stanley,	1 00
Addison Prescott,	10 00	Alfred Sawyer,	2 00
Henry F. Morse,	1 00	Mrs. Amos Buss,	5 00
Herbert F. Moors,	1 00	Elbridge Baldwin,	1 00
George A. Benjamin,	1 00	Benjamin Pierce,	15 00
Frank P. Wellman,	1 00		

JULIUS CUTTER, Treasurer of the Centennial Committee, DR.

To amount of subscriptions, - - $502 00
" paid by F. W. Tracy, for use of Common, 25 00

$527 00

CR.

By paid Geo. W. Foster, - - $25 00
" " for nails and loss on lumber, - 27 12
" " East Jaffrey Cornet Band, - 50 00
" " for Postal Cards and printing, - 22 99
" " for use of tent and expenses on same, 115 64
" " Table Committee, - - 127 70
" " for express, postage and stationery, 8 26
" " for keeping Cavalry Horses, - 16 52
" " amount of subscriptions unpaid, - 1 00
" amount in hands of the treasurer, - 132 77

$527 00

The Committee voted that twenty-five per cent. of each person's subscription be returned, the balance of the surplus to the Treasurer, for extra services.

The Committee of Arrangements tender thanks to Henry C. French, Joseph W. Fassett, and Alfred Sawyer, Selectmen of the town, and to the Table Committee, for their co-operation in making the celebration a success. Also, to the Peterborough Cavalry Company and the East Jaffrey Fire Company, for the very satisfactory manner in which they performed the escort duty.

The Table Committee unite with the Committee of Arrangements in offering thanks to the citizens of Jaffrey for providing funds to defray the expense, and provisions for a free collation. —To H. B. Wheeler, Esq., who furnished us with rooms and lights for our meetings without charge.

CPSIA information can be obtained
at www.ICGtesting.com
Printed in the USA
BVHW04*1209180918
527831BV00013B/883/P